TASTY™
latest & greatest

TASTY

latest &
greatest

everything
you want to cook
right now

CLARKSON POTTER/PUBLISHERS
New York

Copyright © 2017 by BuzzFeed, Inc.

Photographs copyright © 2017 by
Lauren Volo

All rights reserved.

Published in the United States by
Clarkson Potter/Publishers, an imprint
of the Crown Publishing Group, a
division of Penguin Random House LLC,
New York.

crownpublishing.com
clarksonpotter.com

CLARKSON POTTER is a trademark and
POTTER with colophon is a registered
trademark of Penguin Random House
LLC.

TASTY is a trademark of BuzzFeed, Inc.,
and used under license. All rights
reserved.

All recipes originally appeared on
Tasty.co.

Library of Congress Cataloging-in-
Publication Data is available.

ISBN 978-0-525-57564-1
eISBN 978-0-525-57565-8

Printed in the United States of America

Book and cover design by
Stephanie Huntwork

Cover photographs by Lauren Volo

10 9 8 7 6 5 4 3 2

First Edition

CONTENTS

Have a question about a recipe? Download the Tasty app from the iTunes store.

You got this!

Welcome to Tasty. Like you, we live for the joy that cooking brings; the satisfaction that comes from making something you've never before attempted; or even the amazement of picking up that one life-changing hack that will alter your cooking repertoire for life. Whether you're polishing up on how to give pizza dough the glossy sheen of a pretzel or getting your grain bowl on (and seriously, who's not these days?), you've come to the right place. In our world, cooking isn't supposed to be intimidating, or take up your entire weekend, or contain a ton of stuff you have to run around for hours sourcing out. It's meant to be delicious . . . but above all else, it's supposed to be a good time. That's why our recipes are designed to top the charts in taste and fun. Because if you're not enjoying being in the kitchen, what's the point? You, the cooking people of the world, have spoken, and we've answered the call with doable, craveable recipes you will want to make every single day.

LEARN SOMETHING

Like a personal cooking coach, we make it our job to show you exactly what you'll need and how to put it to your advantage in the kitchen. Nothing makes us happier than the gut reaction our recipe videos get online. It lets us know instantly what people think about what we're up to. Were those cheesecake bombs as simple to make as they looked? Yep. Did those chili cheese dog boats taste as awesome as they looked? Double yep. Do we care deeply about what you think, want, and crave? Yes to the third degree.

Cooking with Tasty can also be a daily reminder that it's never too late to teach an old cook (or an up-and-comer) new tricks. It may just be a tiny trick that makes the difference between good to great, or an entire recipe that blows your mind from start to finish. It could be finding a new use for that sheet pan, glass bowl, or skewer—taking the ordinary and making it extraordinary with a little imagination. The idea of cooking as learning is one that drives us every day, and you've told us you feel the same way.

We view it as our job to bring you the very best version of (insert literally every great food on earth), and we take that job very seriously. Our recipes work, but they're also forgiving. A slip of the knife or an extra minute more or less on the stove generally won't derail you—rather, it'll show you that cooking is your friend.

SHARE SOMETHING

Speaking of your friends, don't even get us started about sharing these recipes with them. Food brings people together—that's a fact. Instead of sending a pic of your puppy or kid, how about you send a snap of your lasagna ring? It's a humble-brag *and* some helpful encouragement, all with one press of a button. Then your pic gets passed around, and then some, and then some more . . . Who knows? That blooming quesadilla you made could very well go viral twice—once online and then again in your house.

See, cooking can also be a killer way to bond. Text out a list of ingredients, have everyone volunteer to bring something over, then make something awesome together. Not only do you create moments you can beam out to the world in an instant, you create memories that last much, much longer than that. Remember that time you made pizza bombs out of canned biscuit dough? Or that crazy, impress-your-in-laws ice cream cake that starts with humble packaged brownie mix? Trust us: now you will.

ENJOY SOMETHING

Tasty makes cooking about you, not so much about the recipe. It's about reimagining what time in the kitchen can be. Gone are the days when a recipe took up multiple pages; with this set of winners, you can walk into the supermarket, pick up what you need and, in most cases, be eating within an hour. That's not to say there aren't some special projects here. Magical desserts that reveal themselves layer upon layer? Check. Truffles every which way? Check. Whether it's an of-the-moment recipe like an actual working fidget spinner cookie (we're not lying) or a classic like slow-cooked beef stew, every recipe has the potential for staying power; the deciding factor is you. Unlike so many other things in life, you get to choose which recipes become your time-honored favorites, your go-to's, your dishes that become synonymous with your name and your kitchen. Hundreds of millions of you can't be wrong. That's where the democracy of Tasty comes in. Winning recipes, anointed by fans like you, rise to the top of the heap, powered by likes and comments and shares and smiles.

We believe a recipe can be one of the truest expressions of who you are as a person. Are you an aspiring international jet-setter? A trio of dumplings are right up your alley. Game-day boss? Crispy buffalo wings and cheesy garlic bread to the rescue! Dinner party in the works? Chicken Cordon Bleu it is. It's that hard-to-contain thrill that comes with killing it in the kitchen, the need to share your winning formula for deviled eggs or the revelation that is a boneless barbecue sandwich that keeps the sauce off your fingers and inside your belly. It's that feeling of showing up at a party with a world-beating recipe like glitter-bombed galaxy chocolate bark. You, my friend, are the champion!

Then there are those rainy-day weekends when another hour of Netflix-and-chill routine might make even the most ardent binge watcher look for an off-the-couch activity. Cooking to the rescue! Even if no one initially runs to the kitchen to help prep, once they hear the sizzle of steak, smell that garlic, or see a towering pile of pasta, you know they'll be lining up to help—and definitely holding out their plate for samples. We don't want to just take space on your phone, screen, or bookshelf—we want a seat at your table. That's why we filled this book with an A-game repertoire to ensure you can deliver on the promise of a great dish whenever the urge strikes you.

About This Book

Though Tasty brings people together every day on small screens all over the world, there's still something about having this tangible album of edible greatness at your fingertips whenever you want it. How many times have you been able to convert the "if only I could make that at home?" thought into "I'm going to make this tonight and it's gonna be good"? That's Tasty.

Latest & Greatest is just that: what we've been working on lately and what you've been loving lately. It opens with a chapter of party-friendly food fit for a crowd, like mac 'n' cheese shaped into sticks and fried (we know, right?); jalapeño poppers reimagined as a dip you won't be able to stay away from; and volcano potatoes you could enter into a sculpting contest. Next up? Country-fare like sliders (four types, so everyone's happy); beer can chicken, because it's probably one of our nation's greatest culinary—heck, why stop there?—and historical accomplishments; and Mexican-style tacos that may have you dreaming of opening your own street cart. A whole dessert chapter filled with genius hacks like baking tortillas into bowls and using sweetened condensed milk to make Brazilian chocolate truffles. Classic dishes also take center stage in a chapter featuring pillowy homemade gnocchi (yeah, you can do it!); chicken-and-mushroom marsala; and a pot pie whose biggest demand of you is a pie crust. We don't forget about our vegetarians, with killer dishes that will fill you up with substance and with pride, such as zucchini "meat"balls, a vegan mac 'n' cheese, and buffalo cauliflower that proves you don't need to wing it. Any chapter called Best Ever is, well, the best ever—how could it not be with fried chicken drizzled with honey; super-chewy chocolate chip cookies; and three-ingredient ice cream (we promise—just three!). We also take you globetrotting with a chapter of around-the-world choices that bring far-flung flavors home; think homemade dumplings (you make the dough yourself—go you!); chicken tikka masala (the secret is heavy cream!); and bulgogi, a Korean dish that's easier to make than pronounce (it's bull-GO-ghee, in case you're wondering). Trends are fine and all, but they have to hold their own, and ours do: a cheesecake with a crackling cereal crust is a keeper no matter what the year, and emoji fries are just so darn cute. Finally, you'll flip for our collection of bombs and rings in which everything is either stuffed or circular, rounding out a book full of recipes you're going to make again.

Now that's what we call totally Tasty. Get ready to have a great time.

PARTY

Deviled Eggs Four Ways

EACH MAKES 24 DEVILED EGGS

Boil a dozen eggs in advance and them store them in the fridge for up to a week. That way you've got a world of options for dressing them up. These easy, creative ideas demonstrate that the devil is most certainly in the details.

CLASSIC DEVILED EGGS

2 **eggs**

½ cup **mayonnaise**

tablespoon **yellow mustard**

tablespoon **relish**

teaspoon **salt**

teaspoon **black pepper**

FOR SERVING

Paprika

Fresh **parsley leaves**

1. Place the eggs in a pot and fill with cold water until the eggs are just covered. Bring the pot to a boil, then cover, remove from heat, and let sit for about 12 minutes.

2. Transfer the eggs to a bowl of ice water for about 3 minutes, then peel them and cut them in half. Transfer the egg yolks to a bowl, and set the cooked egg whites aside.

3. Mix all the remaining ingredients with the yolks and transfer to a piping bag. (Alternatively, use a zipper-lock bag with a corner cut off.)

4. Pipe the mixture into the egg whites, garnish with paprika and parsley, and serve chilled.

< **LOADED**

GUACAMOLE DEVILED EGGS

12 **eggs**

2 small **avocados**, diced

¼ cup fresh **cilantro**, chopped

1 **jalapeño**, seeds removed and diced

½ **red onion**, finely chopped

1 **tomato**, finely chopped

2 **garlic cloves**, minced

1 teaspoon **cumin**

1 tablespoon fresh **lime juice**

1 teaspoon **salt**

FOR SERVING

Fresh **cilantro leaves**

Tortilla chips, crushed

1. Place the eggs in a pot and fill with cold water until the eggs are just covered. Bring the pot to a boil, then cover, remove from heat, and let sit for about 12 minutes.

2. Transfer the eggs to a bowl of ice water for about 3 minutes, then peel them and cut them in half. Transfer the egg yolks to a bowl, and set the cooked egg whites aside.

3. Mix all the remaining ingredients with the yolks and transfer to a piping bag. (Alternatively, use a zipper-lock bag with a corner cut off.)

4. Pipe the mixture into the egg whites, garnish with cilantro and crushed tortilla chips, and serve chilled.

LOADED DEVILED EGGS

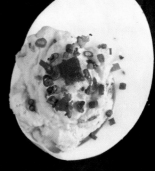

12 **eggs**
½ cup **sour cream**
3 strips of **bacon**, cooked and chopped
¼ cup fresh **chives**, finely chopped
½ cup shredded **cheddar cheese**
Salt and pepper, to taste

FOR SERVING
Bacon, cooked and chopped
Fresh **chives**, finely chopped

1 Place the eggs in a pot and fill with cold water until the eggs are just covered. Bring the pot to a boil, then cover, remove from heat, and let sit for about 12 minutes.

2 Transfer the eggs to a bowl of ice water for about 3 minutes, then peel them and cut them in half. Transfer the egg yolks to a bowl, and set the cooked egg whites aside.

3 Mix all the remaining ingredients with the yolks and transfer to a piping bag. (Alternatively, use a zipper-lock bag with a corner cut off.)

4 Pipe the mixture into the egg whites, garnish with the bacon and chives, and serve chilled.

CAJUN DEVILED EGGS

12 **eggs**
½ cup **mayonnaise**
1 tablespoon **Dijon mustard**
1 tablespoon **Cajun seasoning**
½ stalk **celery**, finely chopped
½ **bell pepper**, finely chopped
1 teaspoon **hot sauce**, or more to taste

FOR SERVING
Smoked paprika
Green onions, sliced

1 Place the eggs in a pot and fill with cold water until the eggs are just covered. Bring the pot to a boil, then cover, remove from heat, and let sit for about 12 minutes.

2 Transfer the eggs to a bowl of ice water for about 3 minutes, then peel them and cut them in half. Transfer the egg yolks to a bowl, and set the cooked egg whites aside.

3 Mix all the remaining ingredients with the yolks and transfer to a piping bag. (Alternatively, use a zipper-lock bag with a corner cut off.)

4 Pipe the mixture into the egg whites, garnish with the smoked paprika and green onion, and serve chilled.

< CLASSIC

< CAJUN

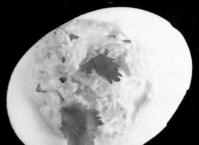

< GUACAMOLE

Carne Asada Fries

SERVES 2

OVEN-BAKED FRENCH FRIES

2 **russet potatoes**

2 tablespoons **olive oil**

1 teaspoon **salt**

1 teaspoon **garlic powder**

1 teaspoon **paprika**

CARNE ASADA

1 teaspoon **salt**

½ teaspoon **black pepper**

1 teaspoon **chili powder**

½ teaspoon dried **oregano**

2 **garlic cloves**, minced

2 tablespoons fresh **cilantro**, minced

½ cup fresh **orange juice**

½ cup fresh **lime juice**

½ pound **flank steak**

1 tablespoon **canola oil**

½ cup shredded **Pepper Jack cheese**

FOR SERVING

Sour cream

Guacamole

Diced **tomatoes**

Fresh **cilantro leaves**

Cotija cheese, grated

Let's face it—getting your fast food fix on is simply too much work when you have to make *two* stops. Fries and tacos mash up in one cheesy skillet to achieve snacking perfection. Bonus: You get to serve them right in the skillet!

1 Preheat the oven to 450°F (230°C). Line a baking sheet with parchment paper.

2 Cut potatoes into wedges. In a large mixing bowl, combine the potatoes, olive oil, salt, garlic powder, and paprika until each fry is fully coated. Place the fries on the baking sheet and bake for 30 to 35 minutes, or until the fries are crispy and golden brown.

3 In a medium bowl, combine the salt, pepper, chili powder, oregano, garlic, cilantro, orange juice, and lime juice. Add the flank steak and marinate for 20 minutes.

4 Heat a cast-iron skillet with the canola oil. Cook the steak for 3 minutes on both sides for a medium cooked steak. Remove the steak and let it rest for 10 minutes before dicing.

5 In an ovenproof skillet, place the baked french fries, Pepper Jack cheese, and diced carne asada, then broil until the cheese is melted.

6 Before serving, top with sour cream, guacamole, diced tomatoes, cilantro, and grated cotija cheese.

Buffalo Chicken Mozzarella Sticks

MAKES 16 STICKS

8 ounces **cream cheese**, softened

2 cups cooked and shredded **chicken**

½ cup **buffalo hot sauce**

2 cups shredded **mozzarella cheese**

1 cup shredded **cheddar cheese**

1-ounce packet of **dry ranch dressing mix**

2 cups **all-purpose flour**

6 **eggs**, beaten

3 cups **seasoned bread crumbs**

Peanut or **vegetable oil**, for frying

Ranch dressing, to serve

No need to wing it here! Any kind of cooked chicken—dark meat pulled off the bone, skinless boneless breasts—will do. Using the freezer as a cooking tool? Genius. While the sticks chill down, you're free to watch the game (or make something else). No bones about it—this recipe kills it for halftime or any time.

1 Line an 8 x 8-inch (20 x 20-cm) baking dish with parchment paper.

2 In a bowl, combine the cream cheese, chicken, hot sauce, cheeses, and ranch dressing mix with a fork until smooth and evenly mixed. Transfer to the prepared baking dish and smooth it with a spatula so that it's spread evenly in the dish. Freeze until solid, at least 1 hour.

3 Working quickly, remove the solid mixture from the sheet and cut into 4 x 1-inch (10 x 3-cm) rectangles. (There should be 16 total.)

4 One by one, bread each stick by coating in flour, then dredging in egg, and then dipping in bread crumbs. Dip once more in the egg, then once more in the bread crumbs, and transfer to the baking dish.

5 Heat the oil to 375°F (190°C).

6 Carefully lower three or four of the coated sticks into the oil and fry for about 30 seconds, until golden brown. Continue this until all of the sticks are fried. Serve warm with ranch dressing.

Chili Cheese Dog Boats

SERVES 8

8 **hot dog buns**

¼ cup **butter**, melted

2 **garlic cloves**, minced

2 tablespoons fresh **parsley**, finely chopped, plus additional to serve

8 slices **cheddar cheese**

15 ounces **chili**, with or without beans

8 **hot dogs**

If making a little bowl out of a hot dog bun to hold bubbling chili and cheese isn't good old-fashioned American innovation, we don't know what is. Every ingredient on its own is a comfort-food classic, but the sum is truly greater than its parts. If you don't have cheddar slices, sub 2 tablespoons of shredded cheese per bun.

1 Preheat the oven to 350°F (180°C).

2 Leaving them attached, place the 8 hot dog buns in a 9 x 13-inch (23 x 33-cm) baking dish. Cut a rectangle in each hot dog bun, making sure to stay 1 centimeter from the edges. Push down on the bread cut-out to compact it tightly into the bottom of each bun, making sure to press down on the bottom edges as well. This will help create a larger space for the fillings and reduce mess.

3 Mix the butter, garlic, and parsley in a small bowl, then brush the buns and their hollowed insides with the garlic butter. Bake for 5 minutes to toast the buns as well as help the sides of the buns firm up so they don't collapse under the weight of the fillings.

4 Place a slice of cheddar cheese inside each bun, then spoon a bit of chili inside each one. Slide a hot dog snugly on top of the chili in each bun, then top with more chili.

5 Bake for 20 to 25 minutes, until the cheese is golden brown and the chili has started to brown. Top with fresh parsley, then slice the hot dog boats along their connected seams to serve.

Fried Mac 'n' Cheese Sticks

MAKES 30 STICKS

8 ounces **elbow pasta**

4 tablespoons **butter**

2¼ cups **all-purpose flour**

2 cups **milk**

1 teaspoon **salt**

½ teaspoon **black pepper**

2 cups shredded **sharp cheddar cheese**

Peanut or **vegetable oil**, for frying

4 **eggs**, beaten

2 cups **bread crumbs**

There are just never enough vehicles for the perfection that is mac 'n'cheese, and these sticks are basic . . . but anything but basic. You get the picture. Pro tip: Make the mixture ahead of time, wrap it well, and freeze for up to a month; when you're ready to use it, defrost it until it's sliceable and carry on with the breading and frying. Cheesy!

1 Bring 3 quarts of water to a boil and cook the elbow pasta. Stir occasionally for 7 minutes, or until al dente, then drain and set aside.

2 In a saucepan over medium-low heat, melt the butter completely and whisk in ¼ cup flour for 2 minutes to create a light roux. Add the milk and season the mixture with salt and pepper. Stir continuously until the sauce fully thickens. Gradually add the cheese and stir until fully combined. Finally, add the cooked pasta and stir until each noodle is coated.

3 Remove the mac 'n' cheese from the heat and pour onto a parchment-lined baking sheet. Spread evenly and freeze for 2 hours.

4 Preheat a pot of oil to 325°F (160°C).

5 Cut the frozen mac 'n' cheese into 3-inch sticks. Dredge the sticks in the remaining 2 cups flour, then the egg, and then the bread crumbs. Fry the sticks for 2 to 3 minutes or until golden brown, then drain on paper towels and sprinkle with salt. Serve immediately.

Grilled Potato Volcanoes

SERVES 6

VOLCANOES

6 large **russet potatoes**

3 cups grated **cheddar cheese**

8 ounces **cream cheese**, softened

1 cup sliced **green onions**

12 strips of **bacon**

FOR SERVING

Sour cream

Sliced **green onions**

If you have a spud and a melon baller (heck, even a teaspoon), you've got what it takes to get these bacon-wrapped potato towers going. Stack, stuff, and grill and you're pretty darn close to potato perfection.

1 Preheat the grill to 400°F (200°C).

2 Thoroughly scrub the potatoes and poke a few holes in them to vent. Wrap in aluminum foil and place on the grill over direct heat to cook for 20 minutes.

3 In the meantime, mix half of the cheddar cheese, the cream cheese, and green onions until well combined. Set aside.

4 Remove the potatoes from the grill and let them rest until they are cool enough to handle. Unwrap each potato and cut off the ends so it can stand up. Using a melon baller or a spoon, carve out and discard the center of each potato, being careful not to make the walls too thin, and leaving a bit of thickness at the bottom. Fill the potatoes with the cheese mixture, and wrap 2 strips of bacon around each one. Secure the bacon with toothpicks, if necessary.

5 Lower the grill temperature to 350°F (180°C) and place the potatoes on the grill over indirect heat for 30 minutes with the lid closed.

6 After 30 minutes, top the potatoes with the remaining cheddar cheese and cook for another 15 minutes. Before serving, garnish with a dollop of sour cream and some green onions.

Shrimp Boil

SERVES 4

SPICE MIX

2 tablespoons **coriander seeds**

2 tablespoons **mustard seeds**

1 tablespoon **red pepper flakes**

1 tablespoon **dill weed**

1 tablespoon **allspice**

1 tablespoon **salt**

3 dried **bay leaves**

8 small **red-skin potatoes**

3 ears of **corn**, cut in thirds

4 **smoked sausages**, such as kielbasa, cut into rounds

2 pounds **shell-on shrimp**

Juice of 1 **lemon**

FOR SERVING

Chopped **parsley**

Cocktail sauce

Melted **butter** with 1 crushed **garlic clove**

Boil, boil, toil and trouble? Not with this recipe, which simplifies this Southern classic and makes it doable for a family night in. The combination of spices along with sausage (use extra-spicy links if you like!) infuses the broth with the flavor that seems like it's been cooking for a good long time. Just make sure to hold off on the shrimp until everyone's at the table: they cook in 3 minutes flat, at which point you're ready to strain and serve—newspaper tablecloth optional.

1 In a small bowl, combine all the spice mix ingredients. Add the spice mix to a large pot with 3 quarts of water, then add the potatoes. Bring to a boil and cook for 15 minutes.

2 Add the corn and boil for 10 minutes. Add the sausage and cook for another 5 minutes.

3 Remove a potato from the pot and check to see if it's fully cooked. If not, continue to cook them until the potatoes are done.

4 Stir in the shrimp and lemon juice. Place the lid on the pot and cook for 3 minutes, or until the shrimp are pink and cooked through.

5 Drain the ingredients from the pot. Serve the shrimp boil on a newspaper-lined table, sprinkled all over with parsley, with cocktail sauce and garlic butter on the side.

Chicken Satay Skewers

SERVES 4

MARINADE

¾ cup **creamy peanut butter**

¾ cup **coconut milk**

4 **spring onions**, roughly chopped

3 **garlic cloves**, peeled

2-inch piece of **ginger**, peeled

2 fresh **Serrano chilies**, roughly chopped

1 teaspoon **curry powder**

1 teaspoon **cumin**

1 teaspoon **turmeric**

1 teaspoon **salt**

2 tablespoons **soy sauce**

Juice of 1 **lime**

8 **boneless, skinless chicken thighs**, diced

SAUCE

½ cup **peanuts**, chopped

½ cup **coconut milk**

Bamboo or **wooden skewers**

If you ever wondered how to make this pu pu platter fave, you're in luck! It starts with a peanutty marinade that benefits from the zing of fresh hot chilies and ginger (you can sub in 1 teaspoon chili flakes and 2 teaspoons powdered ginger in a pinch). Though they're great after two hours of marinating, an overnight soak gets you incredibly flavorful, tender chicken. Bonus: the reserved marinade gets boiled down with creamy coconut milk, creating a thick sauce that just might make double-dipping okay again.

1 In a food processor, blend all the marinade ingredients into a smooth paste; this should make about 2 cups. Reserve half of the marinade and pour the other half over the chicken thighs. Mix and chill for 2 hours or overnight.

2 Preheat the oven to 425°F (220°C). Line a baking tray with parchment paper.

3 Skewer the marinated chicken onto bamboo skewers, then arrange the skewers so their ends rest on the edges of the baking tray, allowing the chicken to be suspended. Bake the chicken skewers for 15 to 20 minutes, until slightly dark brown on the edges and cooked throughout.

4 With no oil in the pan, toast the chopped peanuts on low to medium heat, stirring constantly until the peanuts turn golden brown, 2 to 3 minutes. Add in the reserved marinade and the coconut milk. Stir and cook until thick and very aromatic, 5 to 10 minutes.

5 Serve the chicken skewers with the sauce on the side.

Burrito Cups

MAKES 12 CUPS

FILLING

2 tablespoons **olive oil**

1 **onion**, diced finely

1½ cups **chicken**,
diced finely

Salt and pepper, to taste

2 **garlic cloves**, minced

BURRITO SPICE MIX

1 teaspoon **chili powder**

½ teaspoon **paprika**

1 teaspoon **cumin**

½ teaspoon **garlic powder**

½ teaspoon **cayenne
pepper**

1 **tomato**, diced

6 **flour tortillas**

¼ cup **refried beans**

¼ cup cooked **rice**

½ cup grated **cheddar
cheese**

FOR SERVING

Sour cream

Guacamole

Salsa

Chopped fresh **cilantro**

The secret to this layered and baked dish is three words long: *Burrito. Spice. Mix.* A greatest hits of Mexican flavors, including cumin, cayenne, and chili powder, it turns everything it touches—in this case chicken, rice, onions, and refried beans— into a fiesta. Layering the tortillas into the muffin cups is like an adult art project. Another reminder that food should be fun.

1 Preheat the oven to 350°F (180°C). Oil a 12-cup muffin tin.

2 Heat a large skillet over medium heat. Add the oil and the onion and sauté until translucent, 3 to 5 minutes. Add the chicken pieces, season with salt and pepper, and cook until golden brown, about 5 minutes. Add the garlic and continue to cook for 2 minutes. Remove from heat and transfer the mixture to a bowl.

3 Mix together all the burrito spice mix ingredients, and then add the spice mix to the chicken mixture. Add the diced tomatoes and stir until completely combined.

4 Place the 6 tortillas on top of each other. Cut them into a square shape, and then cut the square into quarters.

5 In the prepared muffin tin, place a tortilla square in each cup and push down. Push another layer of tortilla on top of each in a star formation. Spread some refried beans on the bottom of each tortilla cup, then add cooked rice, and then chicken mixture. Top each cup with cheddar cheese. Bake for 15 minutes, until the tortillas are brown and crispy and the cheese is melted.

6 Serve with sour cream, guacamole, salsa, and cilantro on the side.

Jalapeño Popper Dip

SERVES 4 TO 6

4 **jalapeños** or one 4-ounce can of diced jalapeños

8 ounces **cream cheese**, softened

1 cup **sour cream**

2 cups shredded **cheddar cheese**

1 cup shredded **Parmesan cheese**

½ cup **Italian bread crumbs**

4 tablespoons **butter**, melted

1 tablespoon dried **parsley**

Bread or **crackers**, to serve

Raw jalapeños can be like edible incendiary devices, which is why roasting them is so clutch here. It brings out their kinder, gentler side, perfect for mixing with versatile dip heroes like sour cream and cream cheese—which both serve to further cool the peppers' heat. A bunch of cheese and a crunchy bread crumb topping really make this dip pop.

1 Preheat the broiler. If using fresh jalapeños, cut them in half and remove the seeds, then place the peppers cut side down on a baking sheet. Broil them for a minute or two, until the skins blacken and bubble. Remove from broiler. When cool enough to handle, peel off and discard the outer skin, then dice the peppers. Set aside.

2 Turn the oven to 400°F (200°C).

3 In a medium bowl, mix the cream cheese and sour cream. Add the cheddar cheese, ¾ of the Parmesan, and the diced jalapeños. Mix well. In another medium bowl, mix the bread crumbs, melted butter, the remaining Parmesan cheese, and the parsley.

4 Spoon the jalapeño mixture into an 8 x 8-inch (20 x 20 x 5-cm) baking dish or a medium-sized cast iron pan, spreading evenly. Sprinkle the bread crumb topping evenly on top.

5 Bake for 20 minutes, or until hot and the bread crumbs are golden brown. Serve with bread or crackers.

COUNTRY FARE

sliders four ways 32 steak fajita rolls 34 barbecue beer can chicken 35 tornado potatoes 37 honey-garlic slow cooker ribs 38 mexican-style pork tacos 41 cheesy jalapeño corn dogs 42 buttermilk fried chicken sandwich 45

Sliders Four Ways

EACH MAKES 12 SLIDERS

Buns out, fun's out. Breakfast, lunch, snack, or dinner—you get to decide which slider you want to serve and when. Better yet . . . serve them all.

CHICKEN PARM SLIDERS

12 **dinner rolls** or **Hawaiian sweet rolls**

3 cups shredded **rotisserie chicken**

½ cup **marinara sauce**

8 ounces fresh **mozzarella cheese**, sliced

¼ cup fresh **basil**, chopped

½ cup **butter**, melted

3 **garlic cloves**, finely chopped

2 tablespoons fresh **parsley**, finely chopped

2 tablespoons grated **Parmesan cheese**

1 Preheat the oven to 350°F (180°C).

2 Slice the rolls in half lengthwise. Place the bottom half on a 9 x 13-inch (23 x 33-cm) rimmed baking sheet. Spread the chicken evenly on top, followed by the marinara, mozzarella, and basil. Place the remaining half of the rolls on top.

3 Mix the melted butter with the garlic, parsley, and Parmesan. Brush the tops of the rolls with the butter mixture. Bake for 20 minutes, or until the bread is golden brown. Slice into individual sliders, then serve.

BBQ CHICKEN SLIDERS

12 **dinner rolls** or **Hawaiian sweet rolls**

3 cups shredded cooked **chicken**

⅓ cup **barbecue sauce**

½ **red onion**, thinly sliced

6 slices **Pepper Jack cheese**

¼ cup fresh **parsley**, finely chopped

2 tablespoons **butter**

1 Preheat the oven to 350°F (180°C).

2 Slice the rolls in half lengthwise. Place the bottom half on a 9 x 13-inch (23 x 33 cm) rimmed baking sheet. Spread the chicken evenly on the rolls, followed by the barbecue sauce, red onion, Pepper Jack cheese, and parsley. Place the remaining half of the rolls on top.

3 Brush the tops of the rolls with melted butter. Bake for 20 minutes, or until the bread is golden brown. Slice into individual sliders, then serve.

CHICKEN PARMESAN

BBQ CHICKEN

CHEESEBURGER SLIDERS

2 pounds **ground beef**

1 teaspoon **salt**

2 teaspoons **black pepper**

2 teaspoons **garlic powder**

½ **white onion**, diced

6 slices **cheddar cheese**

12 **dinner rolls** or **Hawaiian sweet rolls**

2 tablespoons **butter**, melted

1 tablespoon **sesame seeds**

1 Preheat the oven to 350°F (180°C).

2 Combine the beef, salt, pepper, and garlic powder on a 9 x 13-inch (23 x 33-cm) rimmed baking sheet, mixing thoroughly and pressing it in a flat, even layer. Bake for 20 minutes. Drain the liquid and set aside the cooked beef.

3 Slice the rolls in half lengthwise. Place the bottom half on the same baking sheet. Place the cooked beef on the rolls, followed by the onions and cheese. Place the remaining half of the rolls on top.

4 Brush the tops of the rolls with the butter and sprinkle the sesame seeds on top. Bake for 20 minutes, or until the bread is golden brown. Slice into individual sliders, then serve.

BREAKFAST SLIDERS

12 **dinner rolls** or **Hawaiian sweet rolls**

9 **eggs**, scrambled

6 slices **ham**

6 slices **white cheddar cheese**

6 strips of cooked **bacon**

3 ounces **baby spinach**

2 tablespoons **butter**, melted

1 teaspoon **black pepper**

1 Preheat the oven to 350°F (180°C).

2 Slice the rolls in half lengthwise. Place the bottom half on a 9 x 13-inch (23 x 33 cm) rimmed baking sheet. Spread the eggs evenly on the rolls, followed by the ham, cheddar, bacon, and spinach. Place the remaining half of the rolls on top.

3 Brush the tops of the rolls with melted butter and sprinkle the pepper on top. Bake for 20 minutes, or until the bread is golden brown. Slice into individual sliders, then serve.

CHEESEBURGER

BREAKFAST

Steak Fajita Rolls

SERVES 3

2 tablespoons **olive oil**, for sautéing

1 **onion**, sliced

3 **garlic cloves**, minced

½ **green bell pepper**, sliced

½ **red bell pepper**, sliced

½ **yellow bell pepper**, sliced

SEASONING

½ teaspoon **chili powder**

½ teaspoon **paprika**

⅛ teaspoon **cayenne**

½ teaspoon **cumin**

½ teaspoon **garlic powder**

½ teaspoon dried **oregano**

½ teaspoon **salt**

½ teaspoon **black pepper**

1½ pounds **flank steak**, thinly sliced

½ cup shredded **Monterey Jack cheese**

Long **wooden toothpicks** or cut **wooden skewers**

Sizzling meat brings out the carnivore in all of us, and it couldn't be simpler to get your steak on than with these cheesy, spicy, pepper-filled pinwheels. Either long toothpicks or short skewers work—just make sure they're well secured so you won't have to slow your roll.

1 Preheat the oven to 350°F (180°C).

2 Heat a large oven-safe skillet over medium heat and add the oil. Sauté the onion, garlic, and bell peppers until soft, about 5 minutes.

3 Combine the chili powder, paprika, cayenne, cumin, garlic powder, oregano, salt, and pepper in a dish, and use the mixture to season the flank steak on both sides. Lay the steak flat on a cutting board with the grain running up and down. Place the sautéed onions and peppers in the middle of the steak, leaving an inch or so on both ends. Cover the onions and peppers with a layer of cheese.

4 Tightly roll up the meat from left to right; this will ensure that you cut against the grain when you slice the meat. Stick toothpicks through the sides of the roll to help it hold its shape, and use a sharp knife to cut in between the toothpicks.

5 Return the skillet to high heat, add the steak, and sear until a nice crust has developed, about 3 minutes. Flip and repeat with the other side. Transfer the skillet to the oven and bake for 10 minutes, or until cooked to your preference.

Barbecue Beer Can Chicken

SERVES 4

SPICE RUB

⅓ cup **brown sugar**

2 teaspoons **onion powder**

2 teaspoons **garlic powder**

1 teaspoons **mustard powder**

2 teaspoons **smoked paprika**

1 teaspoon **black pepper**

2 teaspoons dried **tarragon**

2 teaspoons **salt**

CHICKEN

One 5-pound whole **chicken**, gizzards removed

1 can of **beer**

½ cup **barbecue sauce**

The humble aluminum pop-top becomes a stand for the juiciest chicken on record. Whoever figured that out deserves Nobel-caliber prizes. Get ready to drink half a beer; it'll put you in the mood to use the other half—in the can—for the juiciest barbecue chicken you've ever tasted. Any beer will do, and if you're on the wagon, dump the beer altogether—just fill the can halfway with chicken broth for the same effect.

1 In a bowl, add the brown sugar, onion powder, garlic powder, mustard powder, paprika, pepper, tarragon, and salt, and stir to combine. Use half of the spice rub to season the entire chicken. Cover with plastic wrap and refrigerate for at least 2 hours or up to overnight.

2 Preheat the grill to 350°F (180°C).

3 Remove the chicken from the fridge and season with the remaining spice rub. Pour out half a can of beer. Place the half-filled can in the chicken cavity and stand it upright.

4 Grill the chicken over indirect heat for 30 to 40 minutes. Baste the chicken with barbecue sauce and cook for another 10 to 15 minutes, until the internal temperature reaches 165°F (75°C).

5 Remove the chicken from the grill and allow to rest for 15 minutes before carving.

Tornado Potatoes

MAKES 2 TORNADOES

2 medium **Yukon Gold potatoes**

4 tablespoons **butter**, melted

1 cup grated **Parmesan cheese**, plus additional to serve

½ teaspoon **black pepper**

1 tablespoon **garlic powder**

1 tablespoon **paprika**

1 teaspoon **salt**

Chopped **parsley leaves**, to serve

Wooden skewers

Even those of us with fledgling knife skills will feel like iron chefs after crafting curlicue accordions out of simple spuds. Just thread the potatoes onto skewers, then carve around with a sharp knife. Pulling the potato apart creates all the nooks and crannies you need to season with butter (because, butter!), cheese, and spices before baking to a crisp. Think of it as chips on a stick!

1   Preheat the oven to 325°F (160°C).

2   Microwave the potatoes for 1 to 1½ minutes, and then let stand for a few minutes to cool down and soften. Insert a wooden skewer into the bottom of each potato and gently push it all the way through to the top. Working in a spiral motion from one side to the other, hold a sharp, thin knife at an angle and cut in the opposite direction you are turning the skewered potato, cutting all the way to the skewer. Take your time and work to make a thin, even spiral all the way down the potato.

3   Gently fan out each potato down the length of the skewer, until you have an even gap between the slices. Brush the melted butter all over the potatoes.

4   In a medium bowl, combine the Parmesan cheese, pepper, garlic powder, paprika, and salt. Place each skewered potato over the bowl and shovel half the mixture all over each potato until they are entirely coated. Carefully set the potatoes on a baking pan, letting the skewers rest on the sides of the pan so that the potato is suspended.

5   Bake for 25 to 30 minutes, or until nicely browned. Garnish with additional Parmesan and parsley. Allow to cool for 5 minutes before serving.

Honey-Garlic Slow Cooker Ribs

SERVES 3

1 tablespoon **salt**

1 tablespoon **black pepper**

1 tablespoon **paprika**

1 tablespoon **chili powder**

2½-pound rack of **pork ribs**, halved

1 cup **honey**

½ cup **soy sauce**

10 **garlic cloves,** minced

All we can say about these fall-off-the-bone ribs is OMG. And *easy.* The prep comes together lickety-split, and once they're out of their sloowwww-cooked environment, they've literally made their own salty-sweet, honey-garlicky sauce.

1 In a small bowl, mix together the salt, pepper, paprika, and chili powder. Season the ribs evenly with the mixture, making sure to rub it in on all sides.

2 Add the honey, soy sauce, and garlic to a large slow cooker. Transfer the ribs to the slow cooker and turn them over in the sauce until coated. Position the ribs so they are standing up, with the meatier side down, so the meat is against the walls of the slow cooker, with the bone sides facing in. Cover and cook on high for 4 hours, or on low for 7 to 8 hours. Check after the allotted time to make sure the meat is cooked through and tender.

3 Remove the ribs and transfer to a cutting board. Cut between the bones to separate into individual ribs. Serve with additional sauce from the slow cooker, as needed.

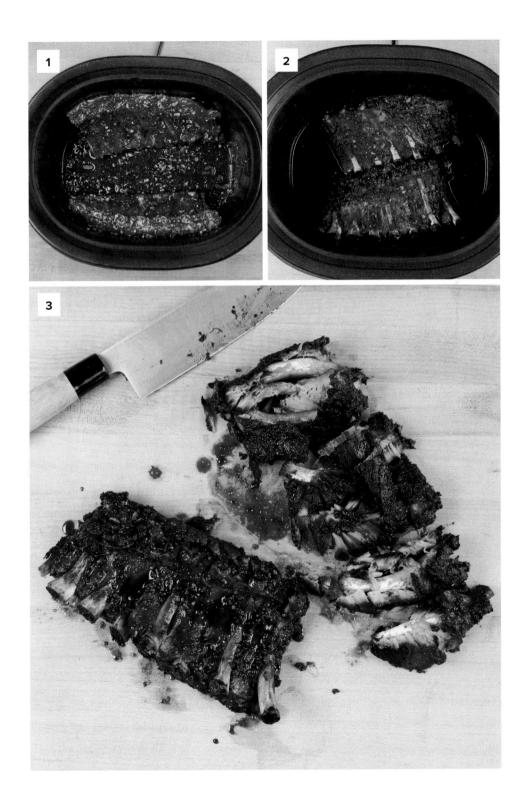

Mexican-Style Pork Tacos

MAKES 10 TO 12 TACOS

5 pounds boneless **pork shoulder**

3 tablespoons **achiote paste**

2 tablespoons **guajillo chili powder**

1 tablespoon **garlic powder**

1 tablespoon **oregano**

1 tablespoon **cumin**

1 tablespoon **salt**

1 tablespoon **black pepper**

¾ cup **white vinegar**

1 cup **pineapple juice**

1 **pineapple**, skinned and sliced into 1-inch rounds

FOR SERVING

10 to 12 small **corn tortillas**

1 **white onion**, finely chopped

1 cup fresh **cilantro**, finely chopped

1 cup **salsa**

1 **avocado**, diced

Lime wedges

1 thick **wooden skewer**, trimmed to the height of your oven

If you're looking for a little tenderness, this succulent pineapple-marinated pork is just the thing. Achiote paste, available at any Mexican grocery store, helps lend the meat its super authentic color and flavor.

1 Slice the pork shoulder into about 1-centimeter slices, then transfer to a large dish or bowl. In another bowl, combine the achiote paste, chili powder, garlic powder, oregano, cumin, salt, pepper, vinegar, and pineapple juice, mashing and stirring until smooth with no lumps. Pour the marinade over the pork slices, then toss to make sure they are coated on all sides. Cover the bowl with plastic wrap, then refrigerate for at least 2 hours or up to 3 days.

2 Preheat the oven to 350°F (180°C). Line a baking sheet with parchment paper or aluminum foil.

3 Place a slice or two of the pineapple on the baking sheet. Take a wooden skewer and push it directly in the middle of the pineapple. Remove the pork from the fridge and push the slices through the skewer, layering one after the other until there is a 1-inch gap at the top. Push another pineapple slice on top.

4 Bake for about 1½ hours, until the pork is slightly charred on the outside and deep red. Rest the meat for about 10 minutes, then carve off thin slices of the pork and roasted pineapples.

5 To assemble, place some pork on the tortillas, followed by a few pieces of pineapple, a sprinkling of onions, a pinch of cilantro, a spoonful of the salsa, and some diced avocado. Serve with lime wedges.

Cheesy Jalapeño Corn Dogs

MAKES 4 CORN DOGS

4 **hot dogs**

4 thin slices of **cheddar cheese**, at room temperature

1 cup **all-purpose flour**

1 cup **yellow cornmeal**

¼ cup **sugar**

4 teaspoons **baking powder**

¼ teaspoon **salt**

⅛ teaspoon **black pepper**

1 cup **milk**

1 **egg**

1 **jalapeño**, minced

Peanut or **vegetable oil**, for frying

Mustard, to serve

Wooden skewers

Meals on sticks tickle us in all the right places. Exhibit A: the corn dog, a fairground treat surprisingly easy to make at home. This version is like cornbread and a cheesy ballpark dog all wrapped into one irresistible package. Note: If the batter isn't sticking, dredge the frozen hot dogs in a little flour for extra adhesion.

1 Place a hot dog on a slice of cheese, then roll the cheese slice around it. Push a wooden skewer through the cheese-wrapped hot dog, then place seam side down on a baking sheet. Repeat with remaining hot dogs. Freeze for 20 minutes.

2 In a large mixing bowl, add the dry ingredients and stir to combine. Once fully combined, mix in the milk, egg, and jalapeño. Stir until the batter is smooth and without lumps. You may need to add 1 or 2 tablespoons of flour; the batter should be thick enough to cling to the hot dog. Pour it into a tall glass for easier dipping.

3 Preheat the oil to 350°F (180°C).

4 Holding the tip of the skewer, take a frozen hot dog and dip it fully into the batter, lifting it out, then rotating it to let excess batter drip off. Using tongs, carefully place the battered dog into the hot oil. Hold it fully submerged for 30 to 60 seconds until a crust forms, then rotate it so that it fries evenly. Cook for 3 to 5 minutes, or until golden brown. Repeat with the remaining hot dogs.

Buttermilk Fried Chicken Sandwich

MAKES 8 SANDWICHES

BUTTERMILK MARINADE

2 cups **buttermilk**

1 teaspoon **salt**

1 teaspoon **black pepper**

½ teaspoon **cayenne**

8 boneless, skinless **chicken thighs**

DILL DRESSING

1½ cups **plain Greek yogurt**

3 tablespoons **fresh dill**, chopped

1 teaspoon **garlic powder**

2 tablespoons fresh **lemon juice**

¼ cup grated **Parmesan cheese**

SEASONED FLOUR

2 cups **all-purpose flour**

1 tablespoon **salt**

2 teaspoons **black pepper**

1½ teaspoons **cayenne**

1 tablespoon **garlic powder**

Peanut or **vegetable oil**, for frying

TO SERVE

Softened **butter** for buns

8 **brioche burger buns**

Butter lettuce

2 **tomatoes**, sliced

With a healthy dose of cayenne in both the marinade and the flour dredge, this sandwich packs the heat along with the crunch. Just the juicy chicken fillet, piled onto a lettuce- and tomato-lined bun, would have been enough to amaze, but the dilly, lemony yogurt sauce puts this one over the top.

1 In a medium bowl, combine all the buttermilk marinade ingredients. Toss in the chicken thighs to coat. Marinate for at least 1 hour in the refrigerator, or overnight.

2 In a small bowl, combine all the ingredients for the dill dressing. Cover and let sit for at least 1 hour in the refrigerator to chill.

3 In a medium bowl, combine all ingredients for the seasoned flour. Dip the marinated chicken in the flour mixture until the chicken is completely covered.

4 Heat the oil to 350°F (180°C) in a deep pot. Do not fill more than half full with oil. Carefully fry the chicken for 7 minutes, or until cooked through. The internal temperature should reach 165°F (75°C), and the chicken should be golden brown and crispy. Drain on a paper towel–lined plate or wire rack.

5 Heat a large skillet. Butter the cut sides of the burger buns, then toast on the hot skillet until browned and crisp. Build the sandwiches with the toasted buns, lettuce, fried chicken, tomato slices, and dill dressing.

SWEET

easy poke cake four ways 48
giant cinnamon roll 52
brigadeiros 56 caramel rose
apple pie 59 tortilla dessert
cups 60 blackberry sorbet 62
white chocolate chip truffles 63
afternoon tea churros 64
strawberry cheesecake
macarons 65

Easy Poke Cake Four Ways

EACH SERVES 12

Don't try to poke holes in this theory: these flavor-drenched cakes are simple, different, and delicious.

CHOCOLATE TURTLE POKE CAKE

1 freshly made **chocolate cake**, prepared from scratch or using a packaged mix

1 (14-ounce) can of **dulce de leche**, warmed

1 (16-ounce) can of **chocolate frosting**

½ cup chopped **pecans**

½ cup **mini chocolate chips**

Caramel syrup, to taste

1 Using the back of a wooden spoon, poke at least 3 rows of 4 holes in the cooked cake, making at least 12 holes total. Pour the dulce de leche over the cake and let it settle into the holes for about 10 minutes. Some of the dulce de leche will still stay on top, which is okay. If necessary, it can be reheated or mixed with a little milk to be thinned.

2 Spread the chocolate frosting evenly on top of the cake. Sprinkle the chopped pecans and mini chocolate chips on top of the frosting, and then drizzle with the caramel. Chill the cake for at least 3 hours or up to overnight.

PEANUT BUTTER BANANA POKE CAKE

1 freshly made **yellow cake**, prepared from scratch or using a packaged mix

4 **bananas**, 2 mashed and 2 sliced

1½ cups **creamy peanut butter**, melted

1 (14-ounce) can of **sweetened condensed milk**

8 ounces **frozen whipped topping**, thawed

½ cup **roasted peanuts**, chopped

1 Using the back of a wooden spoon, poke at least 3 rows of 4 holes in the cooked cake, making at least 12 holes total.

2 In a large bowl, mix 2 mashed bananas, 1 cup of the melted peanut butter, and the sweetened condensed milk; if needed, add extra milk to loosen the mixture. Pour the mixture over the cake and let it settle into the holes for about 10 minutes. Some of the mixture will still stay on top, which is okay.

3 Spread the whipped topping evenly on top. Place sliced bananas on the topping, drizzle the remaining ½ cup of melted peanut butter on top, and sprinkle with the roasted peanuts. Chill the cake for at least 3 hours or up to overnight.

COOKIES AND CREAM POKE CAKE

1 freshly made **chocolate cake**, prepared from scratch or using a packaged mix

1 packet **cookies-and-cream pudding mix**

1 cup **milk**

8 ounces **frozen whipped topping**, thawed

1 cup crushed **chocolate cookies**, plus additional for topping

1 (14-ounce) can **sweetened condensed milk**

1 Using the back of a wooden spoon, poke at least 3 rows of 4 holes in the cooked cake, making at least 12 holes total.

2 In a large bowl, add the packet of pudding mix and the milk, and whisk until there are no lumps. Add the whipped topping and the crushed chocolate cookies. Stir until well combined and set aside.

3 Pour the sweetened condensed milk over the cake and let it settle into the holes for about 10 minutes. Some of the mixture will stay on top, which is okay.

4 Spread the pudding mixture over the cake and smooth it out evenly. Sprinkle extra crushed cookies on top. Chill the cake for at least 3 hours or up to overnight.

BERRY CHEESECAKE POKE CAKE

1 freshly made **vanilla cake**, prepared from scratch or using a packaged mix

2 cups **strawberries**, stems removed

8 ounces **cream cheese**, softened

1 (14-ounce) can of **sweetened condensed milk**

1 cup **blackberries**, mashed

1 cup **raspberries**, mashed

8 ounces **frozen whipped topping**, thawed

Crumbled **graham crackers**, for topping

Sliced **strawberries**, **blackberries**, or **raspberries**, for topping

1 Using the back of a wooden spoon, poke at least 3 rows of 4 holes in the cooked cake, making at least 12 holes total.

2 In a large bowl, mash the strawberries with a potato masher or fork until mashed to a pulp. Add the cream cheese and condensed milk, whisking until there are no large lumps. Add the mashed blackberries and raspberries; stir just once or twice so the colors remain differentiated. Pour the mixture over the cake and let it settle into the holes for about 10 minutes. Some of the mixture will still stay on top, which is okay.

3 Spread the whipped topping evenly on top. Sprinkle graham crackers on top and add sliced strawberries or other fresh berries. Chill the cake for at least 3 hours or up to overnight.

CHOCOLATE TURTLE >

< PEANUT BUTTER BANANA

COOKIES AND CREAM

BERRY CHEESECAKE >

Giant Cinnamon Roll

SERVES 12

DOUGH

½ cup **unsalted butter**, melted, plus additional for greasing the pan

2 cups **whole milk**, warm to the touch

½ cup **granulated sugar**

1 package **active dry yeast**

5 cups **all-purpose flour**

1 teaspoon **baking powder**

2 teaspoons **salt**

FILLING

¾ cup **butter**, softened

¾ cup **light brown sugar**

2 tablespoons **ground cinnamon**

FROSTING

4 ounces **cream cheese**, softened

2 tablespoons **butter**, melted

2 tablespoons **whole milk**

1 teaspoon **vanilla extract**

1 cup **powdered sugar**

If you've never made a breakfast pastry, this would be a great first one to try. Because if a regular cinnamon roll is awesome, this one beats the world.

1 Generously butter a 10-inch (25.5-cm) cast-iron skillet or cake pan.

2 In a large bowl, whisk together the warm milk, melted butter, and granulated sugar. The mixture should be just warm, registering between 100 and 110°F (40°C). If hotter than that, allow to cool slightly before proceeding. Sprinkle the yeast evenly over the warm mixture and let sit for 1 minute. Add 4 cups of the flour to the milk mixture and mix with a wooden spoon until just combined. Cover the bowl with a towel or plastic wrap and set in a warm place to rise for 1 hour.

3 After 1 hour, the dough should have nearly doubled in size. Remove the towel and add an additional ¾ cup of flour, the baking powder, and salt. Stir well, then turn out onto a well-floured surface. Knead the dough lightly, adding additional flour as necessary, until the dough just loses its stickiness and does not stick to the surface. Roll the dough out into a large rectangle, about ½ inch (1.5 cm) thick. Fix corners to make sure they are sharp and even.

4 In a small bowl, combine the filling ingredients and stir to combine. Spread the filling mixture evenly over the rolled-out dough, spreading right to the edges. Using a pizza cutter, make 3 horizontal cuts to divide the dough into 4 long, evenly sized strips. Starting from the bottom, roll the first strip up right to left. Take the first roll and place it back on top of the next strip, starting again on the right side and rolling up right to left, building on the first. Continue with the remaining strips until you have a giant cinnamon roll.

5 Place the giant cinnamon roll in the prepared skillet or cake pan and cover with plastic wrap. Place in a warm spot

and leave to rise for 30 minutes. The cinnamon roll should expand to the edges of the pan during this time.

6   Preheat the oven to 325°F (160°C).

7   Uncover the cinnamon roll and bake for 45 minutes. Cover the roll with foil to prevent the outside from burning, and bake for an additional 35 minutes.

8   While the cinnamon roll is baking, prepare the frosting. In a medium-sized mixing bowl, whisk together the cream cheese, butter, milk, vanilla, and powdered sugar until smooth.

9   Remove the cinnamon roll from the oven and let cool in the pan for at least 20 minutes. Once cool, remove from the pan and drizzle the frosting over the roll before serving.

Brigadeiros

2 tablespoons **butter**, plus more for greasing the plate

1 (14-ounce) can of **sweetened condensed milk**

⅓ cup **cocoa powder**

Chocolate sprinkles

Brazilians are always raving about *their* truffles, and now you'll know why. With three base ingredients (the sweetened condensed milk is key) and a saucepan, you're able to make something impossibly rich, decadent, and customizable. We roll ours in chocolate sprinkles, but you could take them for a roll in crushed cookies . . . or chopped nonpareils . . . or cake crumbs . . . or . . .

1 In a saucepan on medium-low heat, melt the butter and add the sweetened condensed milk. Add the cocoa powder and stir continuously for 10 to 15 minutes, until the mixture begins to pull away from the edge of the pot; it should be very thick. It's done when you run a spoon through the center and it takes a few seconds to melt back into the center again. Spread the mixture onto a buttered plate and refrigerate for 2 hours.

2 When set, butter your hands to prevent sticking, and pinch off a portion of the mixture. Roll it between your hands, until you have a ball about the size of a chocolate truffle. Repeat with the remainder of the mixture; you should have about 12 balls. Coat the brigadeiros in the chocolate sprinkles.

Caramel Rose Apple Pie

SERVES 6

4 **apples**

Juice of 1 **lemon**

½ cup **granulated sugar**

½ cup **brown sugar**

¼ teaspoon **cinnamon**

¼ teaspoon **nutmeg**

1 prepared **pie dough**

¼ cup **heavy cream**

1 tablespoon **lemon juice**

You probably need an expensive tool to make this oversized flower dripping with caramel, right? Nope—just a knife! After soaking the apples, don't throw away that liquid; it becomes the best caramel ever.

1 Peel the apples and place them in a large bowl with enough water to cover. Squeeze lemon juice in the water to prevent the apples from browning. Working with one apple at a time, cut around the core, discarding the core and removing the "cheeks." Slice the cheeks very thin.

2 In a large bowl, combine the granulated sugar, brown sugar, cinnamon, and nutmeg. Stir to combine. Add the sliced apples, stir to coat, and let sit for 30 minutes.

3 Line the pie dough in a 9-inch (23-cm) cast-iron pan, and prick the dough with a fork all around. Chill in the fridge until very firm, 20 to 30 minutes.

4 Working in batches, remove the apples from the cinnamon-sugar mixture by taking a handful at a time and carefully squeezing them with your hands to remove the excess moisture. Place the drained apples in a separate large bowl, reserving the liquid to make the caramel sauce.

5 Preheat the oven to 375°F (190°C).

6 Working from out the outside in, line the apple slices on the pie dough by overlapping each slice to create a rose shape. Roll up one apple slice tightly and place it in the center, creating a bud shape. Cover the pan with foil and bake for 30 minutes. Uncover and bake for 10 minutes, or until golden brown. Set aside to cool for 10 minutes.

7 In a saucepan, bring the reserved cinnamon-sugar liquid to a boil. Once the liquid is reduced by half, 10 to 15 minutes, carefully add the heavy cream and stir well. To serve, pour the caramel sauce over the cooled apple pie.

Tortilla Dessert Cups

MAKES 6 CUPS

TORTILLA CUPS

¼ cup **sugar**

1 tablespoon **cinnamon**

2 tablespoons **butter**, melted

Three 10-inch (25-cm) **flour tortillas**

WHIPPED CREAM

1 cup **heavy cream**

1 teaspoon **vanilla extract**

2 tablespoons **sugar**

TOPPINGS

Fresh **fruit**, as desired

Those leftover flour tortillas in the fridge just paired up with your muffin tin to create a crispy dessert base with endless possibilities. Don't feel like fruit? Swap in toasted nuts. No whipped cream? No problem—use a scoop of vanilla ice cream instead.

1 Preheat the oven to 375°F (190°C).

2 In a small bowl, combine the sugar and cinnamon. Butter each side of the tortillas, sprinkle with cinnamon sugar, and cut into even quarters, making 12 pieces. Place 2 pieces in each cup of a muffin tin and push down so that they create a cup shape. Bake for 13 to 15 minutes, or until crisp. Remove the cups from the oven and allow to cool in the tin.

3 Using an electric mixer, beat together the cream, vanilla, and sugar until stiff peaks form.

4 Assemble the cups by placing a spoonful of whipped cream in each toasted cup. Top the whipped cream with fresh fruit of your choice.

Blackberry Sorbet

SERVES 2

1 pound (about 3 cups)
frozen **blackberries**

¼ cup **honey**, or preferred
sweetener

Those store-bought sorbets have been keeping
a terrible secret from you: you could be making a
better version yourself. Simply whir frozen berries
with honey, freeze in a loaf pan, then scoop your
way to homemade heaven.

1 In the bowl of a food processor or high-speed blender,
   blend the blackberries and honey until thoroughly
   combined. Pour into a rectangular loaf pan and smooth into
   an even layer.

2 Freeze for 2 hours, or until frozen but still soft enough
   for scooping. If freezing overnight, cover with a lid or
   plastic wrap, and let it sit out at room temperature for 5 to
   10 minutes before serving.

White Chocolate Chip Truffles

SERVES 4

3 cups **white chocolate chips**

1 teaspoon **vanilla extract**

½ cup **heavy cream**

1 cup **semisweet chocolate chips**

TOPPING

1 cup **semisweet chocolate chips**, melted

¼ cup **white chocolate chips**, melted

When the chips are down, make truffles. Warm cream and melted chocolate create something the French call *ganache*—but we call miraculous. Once it cools down, portion it out with an ice cream scoop or a melon baller—or, heck, a plain-old spoon will do the trick just fine—before decorating the truffles with candy-shop worthy black-and-white swirls.

1 In a medium-sized pan, combine the white chocolate chips, vanilla, and heavy cream over low heat. Mix until you achieve a smooth consistency. Pour the mixture into a bread pan. Allow to sit in the refrigerator for 20 minutes to cool down.

2 Pour the semisweet chocolate chips into the truffle mix and stir to combine evenly. Place in refrigerator for 1 hour, or until the mixture is solid.

3 With an ice cream scoop, form balls from the mixture. (Refreeze the truffle mix if it begins to thaw.) Keep the truffle balls in the refrigerator while you prepare the topping.

4 Make the topping by melting the semisweet chocolate and the white chocolate in separate bowls. Dip each truffle in the melted semisweet chocolate and allow to dry. Drizzle the truffles with the melted white chocolate and refrigerate. Serve cold.

Afternoon Tea Churros

MAKES 10 CHURROS

1⅛ cups **all-purpose flour**

Pinch of **salt**

2 teaspoons **sugar**

Zest of 1 **lemon**

1¼ cups **boiling water**

½ cup **butter**

1 teaspoon **vanilla extract**

3 **eggs**

Peanut or **vegetable oil**, for frying

Cinnamon-sugar (cinnamon and sugar mixed)

FOR SERVING

Strawberry jam

Clotted cream

SPECIAL TOOL

Piping bag with **star nozzle**

This is one of those desserts you'd never dare try to re-create at home . . . until now, that is. Making the dough is a snap, and though these look most impressive when piped through a pastry-bag star-tip setup, a zipper-top bag with the end snipped off works just fine. When you're ready to fry, don't sweat it if you don't have a candy thermometer—simply tear off a piece of white bread and toss it into the oil when you think it's ready; if the bread sizzles and browns within 30 seconds, you're good to go.

1 Sift the flour into a large bowl. Add the salt, sugar, and lemon zest, and mix to combine.

2 In a large saucepan, add the boiling water, butter, and vanilla. Heat gently until the butter is melted and the mixture is boiling. Turn off the heat and add the flour mixture. Beat quickly until it is lump free, and allow it to cool for 5 minutes.

3 Beat in the eggs one by one until the mixture is thick and sticky. Leave to cool for another 10 to 15 minutes.

4 Transfer the churro mixture into a piping bag with a wide star nozzle. Heat the oil in a large saucepan until it measures 350°F (180°C) on a candy thermometer. Pipe the churro mixture into the oil, snipping the ends with kitchen shears. Cook 3 or 4 at a time for 5 minutes, or until golden brown.

5 Drain the churros on paper towels, then coat in the cinnamon-sugar mix. Serve with strawberry jam and clotted cream for a delicious twist on afternoon tea.

Strawberry Cheesecake Macarons

MAKES 16 MACARONS

3 **egg whites**, at room temperature

¼ cup **granulated sugar**

1¾ cups **powdered sugar**

1 cup **superfine almond flour**

3 drops **red food coloring**

FILLING

8 ounces **cream cheese**, softened

1 cup **powdered sugar**

2 tablespoons **milk**

Strawberry jam

Want to impress guests? This is the dessert for you. If you can't find superfine almond flour, process coarser almond flour.

1 In a medium bowl, beat the egg whites until frothy. Keep beating and slowly add the granulated sugar until stiff peaks form. Sift the powdered sugar and almond flour over the egg whites. Fold the dry mixture into the egg whites, giving the bowl a quarter turn every third fold. Once the batter reaches a lava-like consistency, transfer half the batter to another bowl and add the food coloring. Mix until just combined. Do not overmix!

2 Working quickly, put the white and pink batters into separate sandwich bags. Cut a corner off of each bag and squeeze the two batters evenly into a larger gallon-sized bag or piping bag to create a multicolor effect.

3 Line a baking sheet with parchment paper. (Tip: use a little batter to "glue" down the edges of the parchment paper so it stays put.) In a circular motion, pipe 1½-inch (4-cm) dollops onto the baking sheet. Lift the baking sheet and gently tap on the counter to settle the batter. Let the cookies rest for 1 hour, until they are no longer wet to the touch and a skin forms on top.

4 Preheat the oven to 285°F (140°C).

5 Make the filling by mixing the cream cheese, powdered sugar, and milk in a bowl until smooth. Transfer to a piping bag and set aside until ready to fill.

6 When the cookies are dry to the touch, bake for 13 to 15 minutes, until they have risen. Let them cool for 10 minutes. To fill, pipe a circle of the cream cheese mixture around the edge of a cookie and place a small dollop of jam in the center. Sandwich with another cookie. Macarons are best kept refrigerated until serving.

CLASSIC

Puff Pastry Four Ways

With these four puff pastry hacks, you're thinking your dessert repertoire right out of the box. So feel free to puff to your heart's content!

THE BRAID

MAKES 2 PASTRIES

1 sheet thawed **puff pastry**

6 tablespoons **cream cheese filling**, recipe follows

5 tablespoons **chocolate chips**

Powdered sugar, to serve

1 Preheat the oven to 400°F (200°C).

2 Cut the pastry dough horizontally into two rectangles. Make 5 slits into each side of the dough (making 6 strips on each side approximately ½ inch thick). Leave 3 inches in the center of the dough intact.

3 Spread half the filling in the center of the dough. Sprinkle half the chocolate chips on top. Fold the dough strips down to cover the center diagonally, alternating each side. Repeat with the remaining ingredients.

4 Bake for 15 to 20 minutes, until the pastry is golden brown and puffed. Serve with a sprinkle of powdered sugar.

CREAM CHEESE FILLING

8 ounces **cream cheese**, softened

¼ cup **sugar**

½ teaspoon **vanilla extract**

In a medium bowl, mix the cream cheese, sugar, and vanilla until smooth.

STRAWBERRY PASTRY DIAMOND

MAKES 9 PASTRIES

1 sheet thawed **puff pastry**

9 tablespoons **cream cheese filling**, recipe at left

5 **strawberries**, halved with stems removed

Powdered sugar, to serve

1 Preheat the oven to 400°F (200°C).

2 Cut the puff pastry into 9 equal squares. Taking one of the squares, fold one of the corners to the opposite corner. Leaving a ¼-inch border, cut about three fourths of the way from the bottom of the triangle to the tip on both sides, making sure the cuts do not touch. Unfold the square. Taking the top flap, fold it toward the 2 cuts near the bottom. Take the bottom flap and fold it toward the top edge.

3 Place about 1 tablespoon of the cream cheese filling in the middle, then place a strawberry half on top. Repeat with the remaining pastry squares.

4 Bake for 15 to 20 minutes, until the pastry is golden brown and puffed. Serve with a sprinkle of powdered sugar.

RASPBERRY PASTRY FLOWER

MAKES 4 PASTRIES

1 sheet thawed **puff pastry**

4 tablespoons **cream cheese filling**, recipe opposite

20 **raspberries**

Powdered sugar, to serve

1 Preheat the oven to 400°F (200°C).

2 Cut the puff pastry into 4 equal squares. Leaving a ¼-inch border, make 8 total cuts along the edges of the square, with each cut going about a third of the way through the length of the edge. Make sure the cuts do not touch.

3 Place 1 tablespoon of the cream cheese filling in the middle of the square, then top with 4 raspberries. Take one of the edge flaps and fold it toward the center, looping over the raspberry. Repeat with the other flaps. Place a raspberry in the center, on top of where all the flaps overlap. Repeat with the remaining pastry squares.

4 Bake for 15 to 20 minutes, until the pastry is golden brown and puffed. Serve with a sprinkle of powdered sugar.

BLUEBERRY PASTRY PINWHEEL

MAKES 9 PASTRIES

1 sheet thawed **puff pastry**

9 tablespoons **cream cheese filling**, recipe opposite

36 **blueberries**

Powdered sugar, to serve

1 Preheat the oven to 400°F (200°C).

2 Cut the puff pastry into 9 equal squares. Make 4 cuts on each square, with each cut starting from the outside corners of the square and stopping just short of the center. Take one of the flaps and fold it toward the center. Fold every other flap toward the center until you have created a pinwheel shape.

3 Place about 1 tablespoon of the cream cheese filling in the middle, then place 4 blueberries on top. Repeat with the remaining pinwheels.

4 Bake for 15 to 20 minutes, until the pastry is golden brown and puffed. Serve with a sprinkle of powdered sugar.

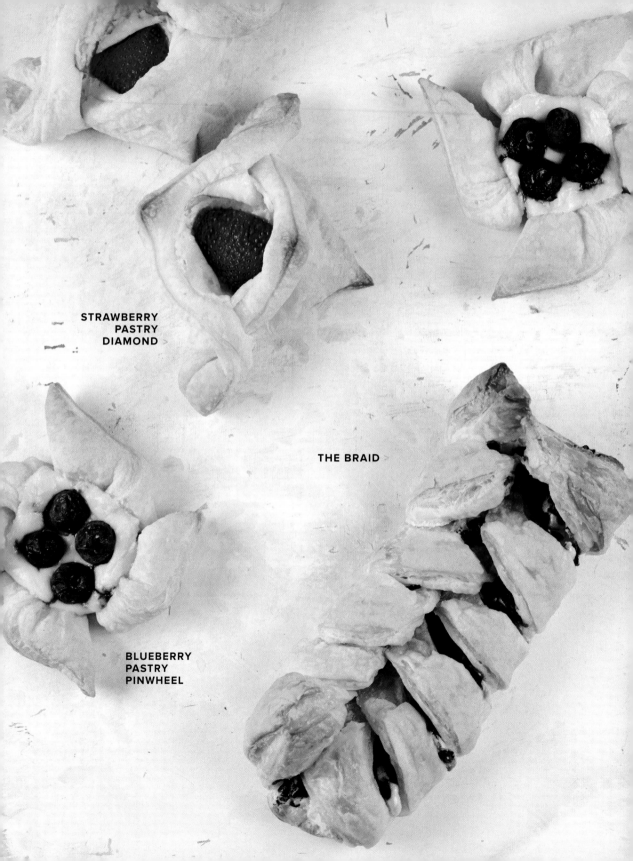

STRAWBERRY
PASTRY
DIAMOND

THE BRAID

BLUEBERRY
PASTRY
PINWHEEL

RASPBERRY
PASTRY
FLOWER

Homemade Gnocchi

SERVES 2

4 small or medium **russet potatoes**

1 teaspoon **salt**, plus more for the water

1 teaspoon **black pepper**

1 **egg**

1½ cups **all-purpose flour**

2 tablespoons **butter**

Sage leaves

The secret to great gnocchi is treating the dough with a light hand. Mash, mix, and knead those spuds as little as possible for the best results.

1 Add the potatoes to a large pot of cool salted water. Bring to a boil, and cook for 20 to 25 minutes, or until a fork can easily poke through one. Drain the potatoes and set aside until cool enough to handle but still warm.

2 Using a peeler or your fingers, remove the skin from the potatoes. In a medium bowl, mash the potatoes until all lumps are gone. Add salt and pepper and mix well. Make a well into the center of the potatoes and crack an egg into it. Whisk the egg briefly. Then, using your hands, gently mix it into the potatoes until evenly distributed.

3 Put 1 cup of flour onto a clean surface and turn out the potato dough onto it, keeping the extra ½ cup close by in case you need it. Working quickly and carefully, knead the dough, only incorporating as much flour as you need along the way until the dough loses stickiness and becomes more solid. Slice the dough into 4 parts. Roll out one part into a long rope, about 1 inch wide, cutting in half and working with one half at a time if the rope is becoming too long. Slice the rope into ½-inch squares and set aside on a lightly floured surface. Repeat with the remainder of the dough.

4 If desired, place a fork on your work surface and slide each gnocchi square from the base of the fork prongs to the top so they make a decorative shape.

5 Bring a large pot of salted water to a boil and add the gnocchi in batches, stirring gently once or twice to ensure they are not sticking. Boil until they float to the top; after another 15 to 30 seconds in the water, remove.

6 In a pan over medium heat, melt the butter and add the sage. Add the gnocchi and toss until lightly golden.

Chicken Cordon Bleu

SERVES 6

4 boneless, skinless **chicken breasts**

Salt and pepper, to taste

1 tablespoon **garlic powder**

1 tablespoon **onion powder**

16 thin slices of **Swiss cheese**

½ pound **ham**, thinly sliced

Peanut or **vegetable oil**, for frying

1 cup **all-purpose flour**

4 **eggs**, beaten

2 cups **panko bread crumbs**

CREAMY DIJON SAUCE

3 tablespoons **butter**

2 **garlic cloves**, minced

3 tablespoons **all-purpose flour**

2 cups **milk**

¼ cup **Dijon mustard**

1 cup shredded **Parmesan cheese**

Salt and pepper, to taste

When a chicken recipe doubles as a magic trick, you know you've got a winner. The ham and cheese inside each crispy chicken rollup reveal themselves when sliced, guaranteeing oohs, ahhs, and yums all around.

1 Sprinkle the chicken breasts with salt, pepper, garlic powder, and onion powder, tossing to coat evenly. On a cutting board, place a chicken breast between two sheets of plastic wrap and pound until about ½ inch (1 cm) thick with a meat mallet, rolling pin, or heavy pan. Remove the plastic wrap and place a layer of Swiss cheese, about 3 or 4 slices, then 4 slices ham, then one more layer of Swiss cheese, another 3 or 4 slices. Evenly roll the chicken, and place onto a new sheet of plastic wrap. Wrap the chicken in the plastic tightly and use the excess plastic on the sides to twist, firming up the roll of chicken cordon bleu as you work. Tie the excess plastic. Repeat with the remaining ingredients, and chill the rolls in the fridge to set for 30 minutes.

2 Meanwhile, preheat a tall-sided pan with 2 inches of oil to 325°F (170°C).

3 After the rolls are set, prepare separate large, wide dishes with flour, beaten eggs, and bread crumbs. Dredge the chicken first in the flour, then the egg, and then the bread crumbs. Place the breaded chicken cordon bleu in the oil, and cook for about 5 minutes per side, or until the outside is an even golden brown. If good color is achieved and the chicken's center is still not 165°F (75°C), place the chicken cordon bleu on a cooling rack over a baking sheet and finish the chicken in the oven at 325°F (160°C) until that temperature is reached.

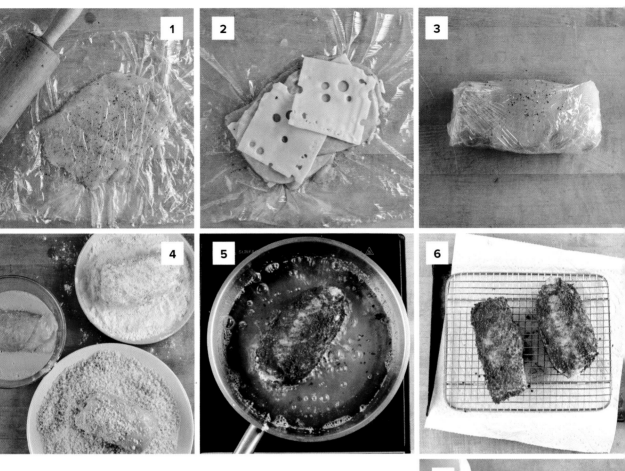

4 Meanwhile, prepare the sauce. In a 1½-quart saucepan on medium heat, melt the butter and cook the garlic until soft. Add in the flour, and whisk for 1 minute. Add in the milk, and whisk until fully combined with the roux and no lumps remain. Continue whisking until the mixture comes to a simmer and has thickened. Add in the mustard, Parmesan cheese, salt, and pepper, and whisk to combine. Set aside.

5 Slice the chicken and serve drizzled with Dijon sauce.

Chicken Marsala

SERVES 6

4 boneless, skinless **chicken breasts**, trimmed

1 cup **all-purpose flour**

Salt and pepper, to taste

1 tablespoon **onion powder**

1 tablespoon **garlic powder**

2 tablespoons **olive oil**

4 tablespoons **butter**

2 **garlic cloves**, minced

½ cup **shallots**, minced

1 pound **cremini mushrooms**, trimmed and thinly sliced

2 cups dry **Marsala wine**

2 cups **chicken stock**

Juice of ½ **lemon**

Fresh **parsley**, to serve

Cooked **pasta**, **potatoes**, or **rice**, to serve

Marsala wine gives this classic recipe its name; if you can't find any, use 1¾ cups dry white wine and ¼ cup brandy.

1 Cut each chicken breast in half lengthwise, then cut the larger, thicker half again horizontally, creating 3 equally thick cutlets. Place the flour, salt, pepper, onion powder, and garlic powder into a wide shallow dish and stir to combine. Dredge the chicken pieces in the flour mixture, shaking gently to remove any excess flour, and set aside.

2 Heat the oil and 2 tablespoons of butter in a large skillet over medium-high heat. Place the chicken in batches to prevent overcrowding. Cook the chicken until golden brown, about 3 minutes. Flip and cook the other side, another 3 minutes. Remove the chicken from the pan and set aside.

3 To the same, now empty pan with leftover oil and butter, add the garlic, shallots, and cremini mushrooms, stirring occasionally and scraping the bottom of the pan until the mushrooms are soft and most of the liquid has evaporated, about 8 minutes.

4 Deglaze the pan with the Marsala wine and scrape all the caramelized bits from the bottom of the pan. Add the chicken stock and lemon juice, and allow the mixture to come to a boil. Reduce to a simmer, and cook until the liquid has reduced by half.

5 Turn off the heat. Add 2 tablespoons of cold butter and stir until the sauce is smooth and creamy. Add the cooked chicken to the sauce and simmer for 5 more minutes, flipping halfway through. Sprinkle with parsley and serve with pasta, potatoes, or rice.

Classic Tomato Lasagna

SERVES 12

BOLOGNESE SAUCE

2 tablespoons **olive oil**

2 tablespoons **butter**

1 **onion**, minced

1 large **carrot**, peeled and minced

1 **celery stalk**, minced

2 **garlic cloves**, minced

1 pound **ground beef**

1 pound **ground pork**

Salt and pepper, to taste

1 (6-ounce) can of **tomato paste**

2 cups **red wine**

1 (28-ounce) can of diced **tomatoes**

RICOTTA-HERB MIXTURE

15 ounces **ricotta cheese**

½ cup fresh **basil**, chopped

1 cup shredded **Parmesan cheese**, plus more to taste

½ cup fresh **parsley**, chopped

1 **egg**

Salt and pepper, to taste

1 pound **lasagna noodles**, cooked

Mozzarella cheese, shredded

Making your own bolognese sauce makes all the difference for lasagna, guaranteeing layers of tomato-meaty flavor between your noodles and cheese.

1 Preheat the oven to 400°F (200°C).

2 Add olive oil and butter to a skillet on medium-high heat. Once warmed, add the onion, carrot, celery, and garlic. Cook, stirring occasionally, until golden brown. Once the vegetables have caramelized, add in the beef, pork, salt, pepper, and tomato paste. Stir to combine, breaking up the pieces of meat, until the meat has browned.

3 Once the sauce is dark brown and starting to stick slightly to the bottom of the pan, add the red wine. Scrape the bottom of the pan with a wooden spoon to release all the cooked brown bits. When the wine comes to a simmer, add in the diced canned tomatoes, and stir to combine. Bring the sauce to a simmer and cook for at least 30 minutes (the longer the better!), and then set aside.

4 In a large bowl, mix together the ricotta, basil, 1 cup Parmesan, the parsley, egg, salt, and pepper. Set aside.

5 In a 9 x 13-inch (23 x 33-cm) glass baking pan, add a layer of bolognese to the bottom. Top with noodles, then spread a layer of the ricotta mixture on top. Repeat with another layer of bolognese, noodles, ricotta, noodles, bolognese, and then top with mozzarella and additional Parmesan. Cover the baking dish with foil and bake for 25 minutes.

6 Remove the foil and bake again for an additional 15 minutes, until the cheese on top has browned and the bolognese is bubbling. Slice and serve.

One-Pot Chicken-Bacon Pesto Pasta

SERVES 4

6 strips of **bacon**, sliced

2 boneless, skinless **chicken breasts**, sliced

2 teaspoons **salt**

1 teaspoon **black pepper**

1 teaspoon **garlic powder**

2 **onions**, sliced

4 **garlic cloves**, minced

5 ounces **spinach**

5 cups **milk**

1 pound **fettucine**

½ cup **pesto**

1 cup **Parmesan cheese**, plus additional to serve

Fresh **parsley**, chopped, to serve

Any recipe that has the words "one pot" in the title is cause for excitement. A sort of alfredo-primavera-carbonara fusion, this one's got flavor for days. You start by rendering bacon until crisp, which creates a base layer of smoky goodness that carries all the way through a creamy, cheesy, garlicky sauce tossed with spinach and chicken.

1 In a large pot or Dutch oven over medium-high heat, cook the bacon until crispy. Add the chicken and season with salt, pepper, and garlic powder. Cook until no pink is showing, then remove the chicken and set aside.

2 Add the onions and garlic to the pot and cook until softened. When the onions are caramelized, add the spinach and cook until wilted. Add the milk and bring to a boil. Add the fettuccine into the boiling mixture and cover. Cook the fettuccine on medium heat until the milk thickens and the pasta is cooked, about 7 minutes.

3 Return the chicken to the pot. Stir in the pesto and Parmesan. Garnish with parsley and additional Parmesan.

One-Skillet Chicken Pot Pie

SERVES 4

1 tablespoon **olive oil**

1½ pounds boneless, skinless **chicken breasts**, cubed

Salt and pepper, to taste

½ **white onion**, chopped

2 **garlic cloves**, minced

1 **Yukon Gold potato**, cubed

2 cups frozen **peas** and **carrots**

4 tablespoons **butter**

4 tablespoons **all-purpose flour**

2 cups **chicken broth**

1 frozen prepared **pie dough**, thawed

1 **egg**, beaten

Whether you make a pie crust from scratch or pick one up from the refrigerator case at the grocery, you've now got the essential item for pot-pie perfection. The filling of potatoes, onions, carrots, and peas—not to mention the excitement of breaking through the flaky crust to reveal the creamy filling—is the cooking equivalent of a cozy set of PJs.

1 Preheat the oven to 400°F (200°C)

2 Heat the oil in a cast-iron skillet. Add the chicken, season with salt and pepper, and cook until the meat is golden brown on the outside and no longer pink in the center. Remove the chicken and set aside.

3 To the same skillet, add the onions and garlic. Sauté until translucent. Add the potato cubes and sauté about 5 minutes. Add the peas and carrots, and stir again. Add the butter and allow it to melt. Sprinkle the flour on top, covering the vegetables, and quickly stir to avoid lumps. Pour in the chicken broth and bring to a boil to thicken the sauce. Season with salt and pepper and remove from the heat.

4 Place the pie dough over the chicken and vegetable mixture, and carefully seal along the edges of the skillet with your fingers. Brush the pastry with the egg, and cut 3 slits in the top to release steam. Bake for 25 to 30 minutes, or until golden brown.

French Pepper Steak

14-ounce **New York strip steak**, or other steak of good quality

2 teaspoons **kosher salt**

2 tablespoons coarsely ground **black pepper**

1 tablespoon **vegetable oil**

2 tablespoons **butter**

1 cup **heavy cream**

⅓ cup **brandy** or **cognac**

1 tablespoon **Dijon mustard**

The revelation in this steakhouse favorite is the chunks of cracked black pepper you smash from whole peppercorns; they're so full of flavor you'll never want to use the powdery stuff again. After you crust your steak in the pepper and pan-sear it, the toasted pieces that remain in the pan are the base for a creamy, spiked sauce that's pan-licking good.

1 Liberally season the steak with salt and pepper, being sure to generously coat the entire surface of the meat. Using your hands, press the seasoning into the meat to create an even coating.

2 Heat the vegetable oil and 1 tablespoon of butter in a large skillet over medium-high heat until just smoking. Add the steak to the pan and sear on one side for 4 minutes. Turn and sear the other side for another 4 minutes, for medium-rare. If the steak has a fat-cap on its side, be sure to sear it as well for 30 seconds to a minute. Once cooked to desired doneness, transfer the steak to a cutting board to rest.

3 Reduce the heat to medium and add the brandy to the skillet. Allow it to cook down for about 1 minute while using a whisk to scrape off any browned bits in the bottom of the pan. Once the brandy has reduced by half, add the cream and continue to whisk until combined. Add the Dijon mustard and remaining tablespoon of butter and continue to cook until the mixture begins to reduce and thicken, 5 to 7 minutes. The final pan sauce should have a rich consistency and be able to coat the back of a spoon. Reduce the heat to low.

4 Slice the steak into ½-inch (1.5-cm) pieces. Pour the cream sauce over the top and serve.

Slow Cooker Beef Stew

SERVES 8

⅓ cup **all-purpose flour**

1½ tablespoons **salt**

½ tablespoon **black pepper**

3 pounds **chuck roast**

1 tablespoon **olive oil**

1 **red onion**, diced

1 **celery stalk**, diced

1 **carrot**, diced

3 **garlic cloves**, minced

1 (28-ounce) can of **plum tomatoes**

2 cups **red wine**

1 **bay leaf**

1 tablespoon fresh **parsley**, chopped, plus additional to serve

1 tablespoon chopped fresh **sage**

Meet our BFF, the slow cooker. Not only does it save us time and mess in the kitchen, it actually makes us feel *good* about lazing out while the beef in this recipe bathes in a luxe, tomato-y, wine-enriched sauce. Oh, and if fresh sage is hard to find, sub in ½ tablespoon dried. Don't worry— your new BFF says it's OK.

1   In a small bowl, combine the flour, 1 tablespoon salt, and the pepper. Rub the flour mixture on the beef, making sure it is covered entirely.

2   Heat the oil in a large skillet. Sear the meat on every side until golden brown. Transfer the meat into the slow cooker. Add the onion, celery, carrot, garlic, tomatoes, wine, bay leaf, and remaining ½ tablespoon salt. Cook on low for 8 hours.

3   Remove and discard the bay leaf. Stir in the parsley and sage. Serve the stew with your favorite side dish, and sprinkle some additional freshly chopped parsley on top.

VEGETARIAN

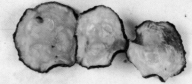

Baked Fruit & Veggie Chips Four Ways

EACH MAKES 1 TO 2 SERVINGS

These crispy, healthy, colorful no-fry snacks are new chips off the old block.

< ZUCCHINI CHIPS

KALE CHIPS

1 bunch of **kale**
2 tablespoons **olive oil**
¼ teaspoon **salt**
¼ teaspoon **pepper**
¼ teaspoon **paprika**

1 Preheat the oven to 350°F (180°C). Line a baking sheet with parchment paper.

2 Remove the kale leaves from the thick stems with a sharp knife, then chop into bite-size pieces. In a medium bowl, top the kale with the olive oil. Mix the seasonings and add to the kale. Toss until fully coated.

3 Arrange the seasoned kale on the baking sheet, ensuring the chips don't overlap. Bake for 10 to 15 minutes, until the edges are brown, but not burnt. Allow to cool to room temperature.

APPLE CHIPS

2 **apples**
Nonstick cooking spray or **oil**
1 teaspoon **cinnamon**

1 Preheat the oven to 350°F (180°C). Line a baking sheet with parchment paper.

2 Cut the apples into ⅛- to ¼-inch (3- to 6-mm) slices. Arrange on the baking sheet. Spray the slices with nonstick spray or brush with oil. Then sprinkle them with cinnamon. Bake for 30 minutes, flipping halfway, until lightly golden brown. Let cool to room temperature.

< SWEET POTATO CHIPS

< KALE CHIPS

ZUCCHINI CHIPS

1 large **zucchini**
2 tablespoons **olive oil**
¼ teaspoon **salt**
½ teaspoon **pepper**
½ teaspoon **garlic powder**

1 Preheat the oven to 400°F (200°C). Line a baking sheet with parchment paper.

2 Cut zucchini into ⅛- to ¼-inch (3- to 6-mm) slices. Arrange them on the baking sheet, ensuring you're not overlapping the zucchini, or they won't dry out properly. Brush the slices with olive oil, then season with salt, pepper, and garlic powder. Flip the slices over and repeat.

3 Bake for 25 to 35 minutes, flipping halfway, until golden brown. Allow slices to cool to room temperature. Slices will continue to get crispier as they cool.

SWEET POTATO CHIPS

1 large **sweet potato** or **yam**
4 tablespoons **olive oil**
½ teaspoon **salt**
½ teaspoon **pepper**
1 teaspoon dried **thyme**

1 Preheat the oven to 400°F (200°C). Line a baking sheet with parchment paper.

2 Cut the sweet potato into ⅛- to ¼-inch (3- to 6-mm) slices. In a medium bowl, toss them with olive oil until fully coated. Add the seasonings and toss until fully coated. Arrange the slices on the baking sheet without overlapping the potatoes.

3 Bake for 25 to 35 minutes, flipping halfway, until golden brown. Allow the slices to cool to room temperature.

< APPLE CHIPS

Vegetarian Grain Bowls Two Ways

Opting for an all-veggie meal may seem to go against the grain, but between the colorful, crunchy veggies and delicious dressings, you won't miss the meat.

ROASTED VEGGIE QUINOA BOWL WITH SOY-MAPLE DRESSING

SERVES 2

2 **carrots**, sliced

1 head of **broccoli florets**

1 **red bell pepper**, roughly chopped

½ head of **red cabbage**, sliced

Olive oil, to taste

Salt and pepper, to taste

Garlic powder, to taste

Onion powder, to taste

2 cups **quinoa**, cooked

SOY-MAPLE DRESSING

¼ cup **soy sauce**

2 tablespoons **pure maple syrup**

1 teaspoon fresh **ginger**, minced

1 teaspoon fresh **garlic**, minced

Black pepper, to taste

1 Preheat the oven to 425°F (220°C). Line a baking sheet with parchment paper.

2 On the baking sheet, season the vegetables and chickpeas with olive oil, salt, pepper, and paprika. Bake in the oven for 15 to 20 minutes, or until the veggies are roasted to your liking.

3 Fill 2 glass storage bowls with 1 cup cooked brown rice each. Then fill with the roasted chickpeas and veggies.

4 Mix the cilantro-lime dressing ingredients and split the dressing between two small glass containers. Store in the refrigerator with the roasted veggie and chickpea bowls for up to 4 days.

5 To serve, remove the containers with the dressing and heat in the microwave for 1 minute. Pour each batch of dressing on top of each grain bowl and mix everything together.

ROASTED CHICKPEA & VEGGIE BROWN RICE BOWL WITH CILANTRO-LIME DRESSING

SERVES 2

1 **sweet potato**, peeled and chopped into bite-sized pieces

½ pound **Brussels sprouts**, trimmed and halved

1 **yellow bell pepper**, roughly chopped

½ **red onion**, roughly chopped

1 (15.5 ounce) can of **chickpeas**, drained and rinsed

Olive oil, to taste

Salt and pepper, to taste

Paprika, to taste

2 cups **brown rice**, cooked

CILANTRO-LIME DRESSING

¼ cup **plain Greek yogurt**

2 tablespoons **lime juice**

1 tablespoon fresh **cilantro**, chopped

Salt and pepper, to taste

1 Preheat the oven to 425°F (220°C). Line a baking sheet with parchment paper.

2 On the baking sheet, season the vegetables with olive oil, salt, pepper, garlic powder, and onion powder. Bake in the oven for 15 to 20 minutes, or until the veggies are roasted to your liking.

3 Fill 2 glass storage bowls with 1 cup cooked quinoa each. Then fill with the roasted veggies.

4 Mix the soy-maple dressing ingredients and split the dressing between two small glass containers. Store in the refrigerator with the roasted veggie bowls for up to 4 days.

5 To serve, remove the containers with the dressing and heat in the microwave for 1 minute. Pour each batch of dressing on top of each grain bowl and mix everything together.

ROASTED CHICKPEA &
VEGGIE BROWN RICE
BOWL WITH
CILANTRO-LIME
DRESSING

ROASTED VEGGIE
QUINOA BOWL
WITH SOY-MAPLE
DRESSING

Zucchini "Meat"balls

SERVES 4 TO 6

4 **zucchini**

1 tablespoon **salt**

1 large **egg**

1 cup **ricotta cheese**

1 cup **bread crumbs**

1 tablespoon **Italian seasoning**

3 tablespoons fresh **basil**, chopped

3 tablespoons fresh **parsley**, chopped

1 teaspoon **black pepper**

2 tablespoons **olive oil**

1 medium **onion**, diced

2 **garlic cloves**, chopped

TO SERVE

Cooked pasta

Marinara sauce

You won't miss the meat in these hearty, flavorful herb-filled "meat"balls—the zucchini is a worthy stand-in that may recruit a few of you to Team Vegetarian. Make sure not to skip the important step of squeezing out the excess liquid from the zucchini after salting; it ensures the balls are nice and firm, not mushy and waterlogged.

1 Cut off the bottoms of each zucchini and use a cheese grater or box grater to shred into a large mixing bowl. Sprinkle salt on top, toss, and let rest in a colander in the sink for 20 minutes to pull out excess moisture.

2 Preheat the oven to 375°F (190°C).

3 Using a dish towel, squeeze out excess liquid from the shredded zucchini. Move the zucchini to a dry mixing bowl and add the remaining ingredients. Stir until evenly mixed, and form the mixture into golf ball–sized balls.

4 Bake the zucchini balls for 30 to 40 minutes or until browned, flipping halfway through. Serve over pasta with marinara sauce.

Falafel

SERVES 4 TO 6

2 (15.5 ounce) cans of **chickpeas**, drained and rinsed

1 **red onion**, chopped

¼ cup **fresh** parsley

4 **garlic cloves**, peeled

1 tablespoon fresh **lemon juice**

2 teaspoons **cumin**

1 teaspoon **salt**

1 teaspoon **black pepper**

½ teaspoon **red pepper flakes**

1 cup **bread crumbs**

Oil, for frying

SERVING OPTIONS

Pita bread

Sliced **tomatoes**

Diced **cucumber**

Tahini sauce

Other than a breaded cutlet, you'd be hard-pressed to find a crunchier sandwich star. Yes, that's cumin you're tasting, and isn't it good? Bread crumbs play a crucial role here, ensuring the crunch that's essential to an irresistible falafel. You can layer it into a pita with fresh salad—or skip the pita, and up the tomato and cucumber quotient for a lower-carb lunch.

1 To the bowl of a 2-quart food processor, add the chickpeas, onion, parsley, garlic, lemon juice, and spices. Pulse the ingredients together until they are just incorporated and form a wet paste. Be careful not to overblend.

2 Transfer the chickpea mixture to a large mixing bowl and add the bread crumbs, mixing until just incorporated. Cover with plastic wrap and refrigerate for 1 to 2 hours, or overnight is best.

3 Remove the chilled falafel mixture from the refrigerator and shape it into 1-inch balls. The mixture should yield 18 to 20 falafel balls.

4 In a large frying pan with high sides, heat about 1-inch of oil to 350°F (180°C). Fry the falafel balls in batches of six for 3 minutes, flipping halfway. Once they are golden brown and crispy, transfer them to a paper towel–lined plate and sprinkle with salt.

5 Serve the falafel as desired, either as a sandwich, salad topping, or over a bed of greens with a side of tahini sauce.

Broccoli Cheddar Soup

SERVES 4

2 heads of **broccoli**

¼ cup **butter**

½ **onion**, diced

¼ cup **all-purpose flour**

2 cups **half-and-half**

2 cups **vegetable stock**

½ cup shredded **carrots**

2 teaspoons **salt**

1 teaspoon **black pepper**

¼ teaspoon **nutmeg**

2 cups grated **cheddar cheese**

Who doesn't love the champion of soups? This version is a little different—it's got shredded carrots for sweetness. You could sub whole milk for the half-and-half if you want to lighten it up a bit, and if you're feeling pressed for time, feel free to use a one-pound bag of frozen, defrosted broccoli florets—just be sure to pat them dry after they thaw.

1 Trim stems off of broccoli heads and chop into small florets. Set aside.

2 In a large pot over medium heat, combine the butter and onion and sauté until translucent. Add the flour and stir until the mixture lightly browns. Stir in the half-and-half and mix until contents reach a simmer. Turn the heat to low and add the stock. Simmer for 5 to 10 minutes.

3 Mix in the broccoli, carrots, salt, pepper, and nutmeg. Simmer for 10 to 15 minutes. Add the cheese and stir until cheese is melted and combines with other ingredients.

Vegan Mac 'n' Cheese

SERVES 4

2 **yellow potatoes**, peeled and cubed

1 medium **carrot**, peeled and cut into 1-inch (2.5-cm) pieces

1 medium **onion**, quartered

½ cup **cashews**

1 teaspoon **salt,** plus more for the water

1 teaspoon **garlic powder**

1 teaspoon **onion powder**

2 tablespoons **nutritional yeast**

1 pound **macaroni**, cooked

Paprika, to taste

If you've ever been skeptical about the whole cashew-as-cheese technique, this recipe will convince you once and for all. Vegetables, simmered until they're soft, are buzzed in the blender with nuts to form a sauce as satisfying as one laden with cheddar and cream. A generous portion of salt is essential here; don't skimp!

1 Add the vegetables to a large pot or Dutch oven of boiling salted water. Cover and allow the vegetables to cook for 10 minutes, until the potatoes are fork-tender. Remove the boiled vegetables and save 2 cups of the cooking water.

2 Add the vegetables, cashews, and seasonings to a blender with half of the reserved water. Blend, adding a few tablespoons of water at a time until the desired consistency is achieved. Pour the vegetable puree over the macaroni and stir to incorporate. Sprinkle with paprika and serve immediately.

Baked Buffalo Cauliflower

SERVES 4

¾ cup **all-purpose flour**

1 teaspoon **paprika**

2 teaspoons **garlic powder**

1 teaspoon **salt**

½ teaspoon **black pepper**

¾ cup **milk** or **milk alternative**

1 head of **cauliflower**

¼ cup **buffalo sauce** or **hot sauce**

2 tablespoons **coconut oil** or **vegetable oil**

1 tablespoon **honey**

Baked, rather than fried, these little buffalo bombs are surprisingly healthy. But don't worry—they don't sacrifice an ounce of their junk-food roots.

1 Preheat the oven to 450°F (230°C). Line a baking sheet with parchment paper.

2 In a large mixing bowl, add the flour, paprika, garlic powder, salt, pepper, and milk, and stir until well combined.

3 Break the head of cauliflower into florets, about 1½ inches wide. Add the cauliflower florets to the batter, making sure each piece is evenly coated. Arrange the coated cauliflower on the baking sheet. Bake for 20 minutes, flipping halfway.

4 Meanwhile, in a small mixing bowl, combine the buffalo sauce, oil, and honey, and stir until evenly combined. Brush the buffalo sauce mixture on the cauliflower and bake for an additional 20 minutes.

Baked Ratatouille

SERVES 8

VEGGIES

2 **eggplants**

6 **Roma tomatoes**

2 **yellow squash**

2 **zucchini**

SAUCE

2 tablespoons **olive oil**

1 **onion**, diced

4 **garlic cloves**, minced

1 **red bell pepper,** diced

1 **yellow bell pepper**, diced

Salt and pepper, to taste

1 can (28 ounces) **crushed tomatoes**

2 tablespoons chopped fresh **basil** (from 8 to 10 leaves)

HERB SEASONING

2 tablespoons chopped fresh **basil** (from 8 to 10 leaves)

1 teaspoon minced **garlic**

2 tablespoons chopped fresh **parsley**

2 teaspoons fresh **thyme**

Salt and pepper, to taste

4 tablespoons **olive oil**

Most vegetable side dishes don't have entire movies named after them—but this one does. Maybe it's the fact that it's French that makes it feel exotic—but it uses American ingredients you can find in any store. This recipe has an extra advantage: instead of slaving over a saucepan, you just layer, cover, and bake. Maybe it's time for a sequel.

1 Preheat the oven to 375°F (190°C).

2 Slice the eggplants, tomatoes, squash, and zucchini into approximately ¹⁄₁₆-inch rounds, and set aside.

3 Heat 2 tablespoons of olive oil in a 12-inch (30-cm) oven-safe pan. Sauté the onions, garlic, and bell peppers until soft. Season with salt and pepper, then add the crushed tomatoes. Stir until the ingredients are fully incorporated. Turn off the heat, then add the basil. Stir once more, then smooth the surface of the sauce with a spatula.

4 Arrange the sliced veggies in alternating patterns (for example, eggplant, tomato, squash, zucchini) on top of the sauce from the outer edge to the middle of the pan. Season with salt and pepper. Cover the pan with tin foil and bake for 40 minutes. Uncover, then bake for an additional 20 minutes. The vegetables should be soft.

5 Mix the herb seasoning ingredients and pour over the cooked ratatouille.

6 Serve while hot as a main dish or side. The ratatouille is also excellent the next day—cover with foil and reheat in a 350°F (180°C) oven for 15 minutes or simply microwave to desired temperature.

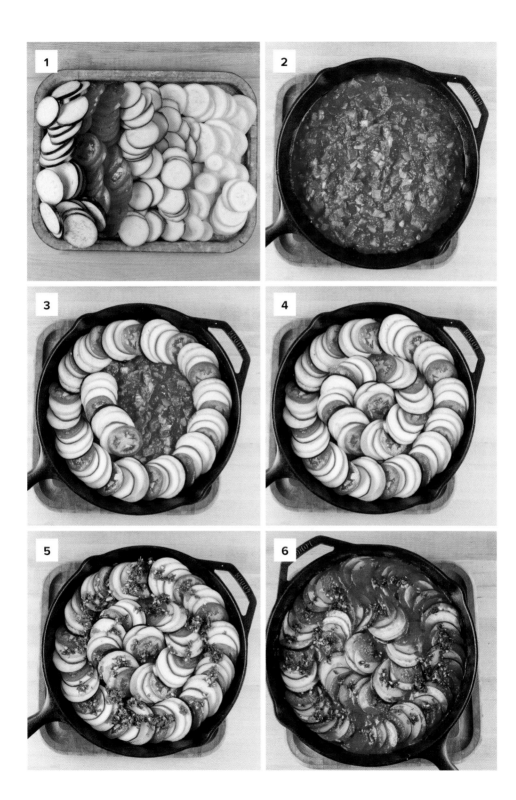

Peanut Noodle Pasta Salad

SERVES 8

½ cup **peanut butter**, creamy

¼ cup **soy sauce**

¼ cup **rice vinegar**

1 tablespoon **sesame oil**

2 tablespoons **Sriracha sauce**

1 tablespoon minced **ginger**

3 **garlic cloves**, minced

2 tablespoons **brown sugar**

Salt

1 box **whole grain linguine**, or any pasta will do

2 large **carrots**, julienned

2 **cucumbers**, shaved using a vegetable peeler

1 **red bell pepper**, thinly sliced into strips

1 **yellow bell pepper**, thinly sliced into strips

3 **green onions**, sliced

¼ cup fresh **cilantro**, chopped

¼ cup **peanuts**, chopped

Peanut butter moves out of the jar and straight into this Chinese takeout mainstay. The advantage of making it at home is yours won't be gloppy or gluey, as the order-in variety can be. The sauce is sweet, spicy, salty, and sublime, giving both the slippery noodles and crunchy vegetables an unforgettable flavor boost.

1 In a medium bowl, whisk together the peanut butter, soy sauce, rice vinegar, sesame oil, Sriracha, ginger, garlic, brown sugar, and ¼ cup water.

2 Bring a large pot of salted water to a boil. Cook the pasta according to instructions on the box. Drain and run under cold water to cool.

3 Combine the pasta with the sliced vegetables. Pour the dressing over the pasta and vegetables and mix well. Cover and chill for at least 1 hour, or overnight. To serve, garnish with chopped cilantro and peanuts.

BEST EVER

Easiest 3-Ingredient Desserts Ever Four Ways

If you can count to three, you can make any of these stellar desserts. We've got you, sweetness.

EASY PEANUT BUTTER S'MORES DIP

SERVES 4

1 pound **mini peanut butter cups**

1 pound large **marshmallows**

15 **graham crackers**

1 Preheat the oven to 350°F (180°C).

2 Place the peanut butter cups in an even layer on the bottom of a large skillet or an oven-safe skillet. Place the marshmallows in a single layer on top. Bake for 20 minutes, until the marshmallows are golden brown. Serve with graham crackers for dipping.

EASY TRIPLE DECKER BOX BROWNIES

SERVES 4

1 (16-ounce) tube of **cookie dough**

16 **chocolate sandwich cookies**

½ **box brownie batter**, prepared per package instructions

1 Preheat the oven to 350°F (180°C).

2 Press the cookie dough in an even layer on the bottom of a 9 x 9-inch (23 x 23-cm) square baking pan. Place the cookies in an even layer on top of the cookie dough. Pour the brownie batter on top, spreading it evenly over the cookies. Bake for 45 to 50 minutes, until a toothpick inserted inside comes out clean. Cool, slice, then serve.

EASY PALMIER COOKIES

SERVES 4

1 sheet **puff pastry**, thawed

4 tablespoons **butter**, melted

1 cup **cane sugar**

1 Unwrap the puff pastry. Using your hands or a rolling pin, flatten out the seams if your puff pastry has them, making an even rectangle. Brush the melted butter evenly over the puff pastry. Sprinkle half the sugar on the pastry, then spread it around evenly. Using a rolling pin, roll the pastry into a tall rectangle, pressing the sugar into the pastry. Flip the pastry, then repeat the process, brushing with butter and rolling in the rest of the sugar.

2 Tightly roll the bottom of the pastry toward the middle, stopping at the center, and roll the top of pastry to meet at the center. The rolls should be the same size. Wrap in plastic wrap and chill for about 30 minutes.

3 Preheat the oven to 425°F (220°C).

4 Remove the plastic wrap and push one of the rolls directly on top of the other. Trim off the uneven ends of the pastry, then slice into ½-inch cookie rounds. They should look like smushed hearts. Place the slices on a baking tray lined with parchment paper about 2 inches apart to allow for expansion. Bake for 15 minutes, flipping them halfway, until the sugar is caramelized and the cookies are golden brown.

EASY COOKIES AND CREAM TRUFFLES

SERVES 6

36 **chocolate sandwich cookies**

8 ounces **cream cheese**, softened

12 ounces **white chocolate**, melted

1 In a food processor, finely crush the cookies. Reserve about 2 tablespoons of the mixture for sprinkling on top of the truffles. In a large bowl, combine the cookie crumbs and cream cheese, stirring until evenly mixed. Chill the mixture for about an hour, or until the mixture can be rolled into a ball and hold its shape.

2 Divide and roll the mixture into golf ball–sized balls. Dip a truffle in the melted white chocolate and place on a baking tray lined with parchment paper. Sprinkle some of the cookie crumbs on top of the truffle before the chocolate hardens. Repeat with the rest of the truffles, reheating the chocolate if necessary.

EASY PEANUT
BUTTER
S'MORES
DIP

EASY COOKIES
AND CREAM
TRUFFLES

**EASY TRIPLE
DECKER
BOX
BROWNIES**

**EASY PALMIER
COOKIES**

Softest Sugar Cookies Ever

MAKES 24 COOKIES

COOKIES

3½ cups **all-purpose flour**

1½ teaspoons **baking soda**

¼ teaspoon **salt**

1 cup **unsalted butter,** softened

¾ cup **granulated sugar**

½ cup **sour cream**

1 **egg**

1 teaspoon **vanilla extract**

FROSTING

½ cup **unsalted butter,** softened

2 cups **powdered sugar**

2 tablespoons **milk**

Why slice-and-bake when you can make-and-bake? The easy, glossy topping is the icing on the cake (or, in this case, on the cookie).

1 Preheat the oven to 300°F (150°C). Line a baking sheet with parchment paper.

2 In a medium bowl, add the flour, baking soda, and salt. Whisk to combine. Set aside.

3 In a large bowl, mix the butter, sugar, and cream together using a hand mixer until light and fluffy, about 5 minutes. Add the egg and mix until fully incorporated. Add the sour cream and vanilla and mix until creamy. Add the flour mixture, one third at a time, until fully combined.

4 Lightly flour your work surface and turn out the dough. Press the dough together into a disc shape and wrap in plastic wrap. Chill for 1 hour in the refrigerator.

5 Remove the plastic wrap from the dough and lightly flour your surface. Roll out the dough about ½-inch thick. Cut out circles using a glass or cookie cutter.

6 Transfer cookies to the prepared baking sheet, leaving about 1 inch in between cookies. Bake for 8 minutes, until the cookie bottoms are golden brown and the tops are pale. Let cookies cool on a wire rack.

7 Make the frosting. In a bowl, beat the butter with a hand mixer until fluffy. Sift in the powdered sugar and mix until incorporated. Add the milk and continue to beat until the mixture is smooth and velvety. Frost the cooled cookies and decorate as you wish.

Fudgiest Brownies Ever

MAKES 9 BROWNIES

8 ounces **good-quality chocolate**

¾ cup **butter**, melted

1¼ cups **sugar**

2 **eggs**

2 teaspoons **vanilla extract**

¾ cup **all-purpose flour**

¼ cup **cocoa powder**

1 teaspoon **salt**

Saying something is the best *anything* ever is a lot to live up to, but these brownies truly are the epitome of dessert goodness. Their superiority depends on two smart moves: skimping on the flour and borderline overdoing it on chocolate. While we're on the subject of chocolate, use the best semisweet or bittersweet chocolate you can find—it's worth it.

1 Preheat the oven to 350°F (180°C). Line an 8-inch (20-cm) square baking dish with parchment paper.

2 Chop the chocolate into chunks. Melt half of the chocolate in a microwave in 20-second intervals, saving the other half for later.

3 In a large bowl, mix the butter and sugar, then beat in the eggs and vanilla for 1 to 2 minutes, until the mixture becomes fluffy and light in color. Whisk in the melted chocolate (make sure the chocolate is not too hot or else the eggs will cook), then sift in the flour, cocoa powder, and salt. Fold the dry ingredients into the wet ingredients, being careful not to overmix as this will cause the brownies to be more cake-like in texture. Fold in the chocolate chunks, then transfer the batter into the prepared baking dish.

4 Bake for 20 to 25 minutes, depending on how fudgy you like your brownies, then cool completely. Slice, and serve with a nice cold glass of milk!

Cheesiest Garlic Bread Ever

SERVES 4

⅓ stick **butter**, softened

⅓ cup fresh **parsley**, finely chopped

⅓ cup **green onions,** sliced

⅓ cup fresh **oregano**, minced

5 **garlic cloves**, minced

½ cup shredded **cheddar cheese**

½ cup chopped fresh **mozzarella cheese**

½ cup shredded **Parmesan cheese**

One 8-inch **baguette**

In the category of irresistible foods, this one rises to the top. Three—count 'em—types of cheese star in a buttery, herb-flecked spread that covers a split loaf of bread like white on rice. Baked until bubbly, it's hands down the cheesiest, most decadent version of garlic bread you've ever tasted.

1 Preheat the oven to 400°F (200°C). Line a baking sheet with parchment paper.

2 In a bowl, combine the butter, herbs, garlic, and cheeses, and mix until smooth.

3 Slice the baguette in half lengthwise, then spread the butter mixture to your liking evenly on the cut sides of the baguette. (Any leftover mix can be frozen for up to 1 month.) Place the baguette on the prepared baking sheet and bake for 15 minutes, until cheese is bubbly and starting to brown on the edges. Slice, cool, and serve!

Chewiest Chocolate Chip Cookies Ever

MAKES 8 TO 12 COOKIES

½ cup **granulated sugar**

¾ cup **brown sugar**, packed

1 teaspoon **salt**

½ cup **butter**, melted

1 **egg**

1 teaspoon **vanilla extract**

1¼ cups **all-purpose flour**

½ teaspoon **baking soda**

4 ounces **milk** or **semisweet chocolate chunks**

4 ounces **dark chocolate chunks**

Are you a crispy or a chewy? Either way, you'll fall in love with these luscious, chocolatey cookies from the first bite. Melted butter is one secret to their tender texture and slightly flatter shape. Using a generous amount of brown sugar, being careful not to overmix the batter, and underbaking the cookies slightly all work in these cookies' favor.

1 In a large bowl, whisk together the sugars, salt, and butter until a paste has formed with no lumps. Whisk in the egg and vanilla, beating until light ribbons fall off the whisk and remain for a short while before falling back into the mixture. Sift in the flour and baking soda, then fold the mixture with a spatula. (Be careful not to overmix, which would cause the gluten in the flour to toughen, resulting in cakier cookies.) Fold in the chocolate chunks evenly, then chill the dough for at least 30 minutes. For a more intense toffee-like flavor and deeper color, chill the dough overnight. The longer the dough rests, the more complex its flavor will be.

2 Preheat the oven to 350°F (180°C). Line a baking sheet with parchment paper.

3 Scoop the dough with an ice cream scoop onto the prepared baking sheet, leaving at least 4 inches (10 cm) of space between cookies and 2 inches (5 cm) of space from the edges of the pan so that the cookies can spread evenly.

4 Bake for 12 to 15 minutes, or until the edges have started to barely brown. Cool completely, and enjoy!

Crispiest Buffalo Wings Ever

SERVES 4

¾ cup **cornstarch**

2 pounds **chicken wings**, rinsed and patted dry

¼ cup **all-purpose flour**

1 teaspoon **paprika**

1 teaspoon **garlic powder**

1 teaspoon **cayenne pepper**

2 teaspoons **baking powder**

2 teaspoons **salt**

1 teaspoon **black pepper**

Peanut or **vegetable oil**, for frying

½ cup **buffalo sauce**

Ranch or **blue cheese dip**, to serve

Celery sticks, to serve

Who knew plain old cornstarch made the crispiest, crunchiest fried things ever? Now, you do. You're welcome.

1 In a bowl, toss ¼ cup of cornstarch and the chicken wings together until fully coated. Transfer the wings to a wire rack and allow them to rest and dry out for 20 minutes, ideally in the fridge if you have space!

2 In a mixing bowl, whisk together the remaining ½ cup of cornstarch, the flour, paprika, garlic powder, cayenne, baking powder, salt, and pepper. Gradually whisk in ⅔ cup of water, breaking up any lumps and mixing until smooth. The batter should be slightly runny.

3 Heat oil in a pot to 350°F (180°C).

4 Coat the chicken wings in the batter, shaking off any excess. Add the wings to the pot in batches, cooking for 8 to 10 minutes, until golden brown. Once cooked, transfer the chicken to a wire rack set on top of a paper towel–lined sheet pan.

5 Transfer the chicken to a clean bowl, and drizzle with the buffalo sauce, tossing to coat. Transfer to a serving plate. Serve with either ranch or blue cheese dressing and celery sticks.

Juiciest Honey-Glazed Fried Chicken Ever

SERVES 8

2 tablespoons **salt**

3 tablespoons **black pepper**

2 tablespoons **onion powder**

2 tablespoons **garlic powder**

3 tablespoons **paprika**

2 tablespoons ground **cumin**

2 tablespoons dried **oregano**

2 teaspoons **cayenne**

3 cups **all-purpose flour**

4 bone-in, skin-on **chicken thighs**

4 bone-in, skin-on **chicken drumsticks**

3 cups **buttermilk**

Peanut or **vegetable oil**, for frying

Honey, to serve

Lean on your pantry full of dried-spice staples to season this chicken. Soaking the chicken in buttermilk is one of the oldest tricks in the book, and for good reason: it tenderizes the meat and is the perfect glue for a flour dredge, yielding the best honey-drizzled chicken ever.

1 In a medium bowl, add the salt, pepper, onion powder, garlic powder, paprika, cumin, oregano, and cayenne and mix until combined. In another bowl, combine half of the spice mix with the flour, mixing until the spices are evenly distributed throughout the flour.

2 Add the chicken to a bowl, and sprinkle the remaining spice blend over it. Mix until all the chicken pieces are evenly coated. Pour the buttermilk over the chicken, and stir until the residual spices from the chicken have blended in with the buttermilk to create a light orange color. Marinate the chicken in the fridge for 2 hours, or overnight.

3 Heat oil to about 325°F (160°C) in a large cast-iron skillet.

4 Dredge each piece of chicken into the flour, shaking off any excess. Dip them back into the buttermilk mixture, then back into the flour. Make sure to shake off excess flour or it'll burn while frying.

5 Fry 3 or 4 chicken pieces at a time, occasionally turning them over. Cook for 10 to 12 minutes, until golden brown, crispy, and the internal temperature reaches 165°F (75°C). Rest the cooked chicken pieces on a wire rack to let excess oil drain off.

6 Drizzle the chicken with honey, then serve.

Creamiest Ice Cream Ever Two Ways

Heavy cream and dark chocolate are the common denominators in these two easy, breezy variations on America's fave dessert. One folds in egg yolks for richer, denser results, but both recipes make ice cream that's on par with the parlor.

3-INGREDIENT CHOCOLATE ICE CREAM

SERVES 6

10 ounces **bittersweet chocolate**, melted

1 (14-ounce) can of **sweetened condensed milk**

1 pint **heavy whipping cream**

1 Place a large glass or stainless-steel mixing bowl in the freezer for at least 15 minutes.

2 In a small microwave-safe bowl, combine the chocolate and sweetened condensed milk. Microwave for 30 seconds at a time, stirring after each, until melted. Set aside to cool slightly.

3 Remove the mixing bowl from the freezer and add the heavy whipping cream. Beat with an electric mixer until the cream begins to form firm peaks. Fold a large spoonful of the whipped cream into the chocolate mixture to thin it out. Fold the chocolate mixture back into the whipped cream mixture until just combined, being careful not to overmix, which will deflate the whipped cream.

4 Pour into a loaf pan or 9 x 9-inch (23 x 23 cm) baking pan. Cover and freeze until firm, about 4 hours.

REAL-DEAL CHOCOLATE ICE CREAM

SERVES 10

2 cups **heavy whipping cream**

1½ cups **whole milk**

¾ cup **sugar**

¼ cup **cocoa powder**

¼ teaspoon **salt**

7 **egg yolks**

10 ounces **bittersweet chocolate**, melted and cooled slightly

SPECIAL EQUIPMENT
Ice cream maker

1 In a medium saucepan over medium heat, add the whipping cream, milk, ½ cup of sugar, the cocoa powder, and salt. Heat the mixture, stirring occasionally, until the sugar has dissolved and the mixture is hot and steaming (but not quite at a simmer). The temperature should read 175 to 180°F (80 to 82°C). Remove from heat.

2 While the milk mixture is heating, whisk together the remaining ¼ cup of sugar with the egg yolks in a small mixing bowl. Whisk in the melted chocolate until smooth.

3 Add a large splash, about 1 cup, of the hot milk mixture to the eggs and chocolate, and whisk until smooth. Pour the egg mixture back into the saucepan and return to heat. Cook over low-medium heat for 5 to 10 minutes, stirring constantly, until the mixture has thickened and begins to steam, or until the mixture reaches 175 to 180°F (80 to 82°C) on an instant-read thermometer. Do not let the mixture boil.

4 Remove from heat and pour the mixture through a fine-mesh sieve into a large mixing bowl. Stir in the vanilla. Allow the custard to cool slightly before covering with plastic wrap and chilling in the refrigerator for at least 4 hours, preferably overnight.

5 Once the custard has cooled, transfer to an ice cream maker and follow the manufacturer's directions for use. Serve immediately or transfer the finished custard to a loaf pan or a 9 x 9-inch (23 x 23 cm) baking pan. Cover and freeze until firm.

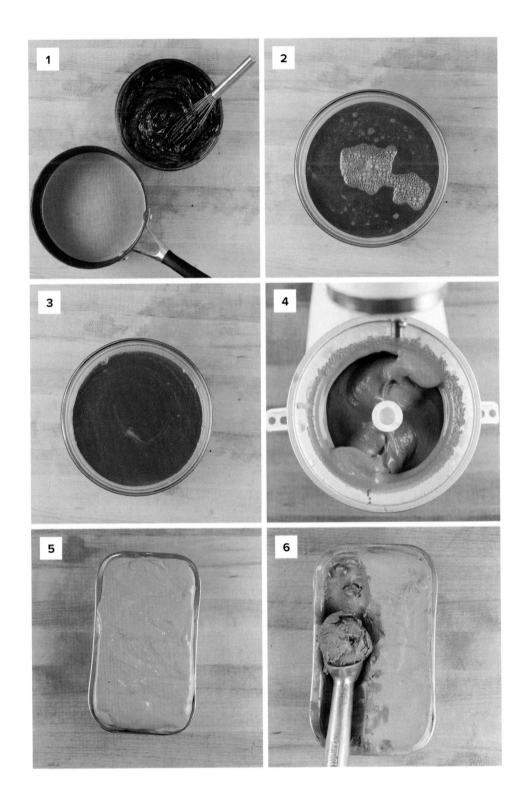

REAL-DEAL
CHOCOLATE
ICE CREAM

AROUND THE WORLD

Dumplings Three Ways

MAKES 24 TO 32 DUMPLINGS

Preparing your own dumpling dough is simple and cheap, and you will feel like a pro. These three filling suggestions—veggie, pork, and shrimp—are just the beginning. Once you get the hang of the of the dough, you could improvise on fillings for the rest of your dumpling-loving life.

4 cups **all-purpose flour**

2 teaspoons **salt**

1¼ cups **warm water**

2 cups **red cabbage**

2 cups **green onions**, sliced

6 **garlic cloves**, minced

4 tablespoons **ginger**, minced

2 tablespoons **soy sauce**

2 tablespoons **sesame oil**

½ pound **ground pork**

½ teaspoon **black pepper**

¾ cup **mushrooms**, diced

¾ cup **carrots**, diced

½ pound **shrimp**, peeled and deveined

¼ cup **vegetable oil**

DIPPING SAUCE

¼ cup **soy sauce**

¼ cup **rice wine vinegar**

1 teaspoon **sesame oil**

1 teaspoon crushed **red pepper flakes**

1 Combine the flour, 1 teaspoon salt, and the warm water and mix until well combined. Roll out the dough on a floured surface and knead until smooth. Separate the dough into 4 equal parts.

2 Roll out 1 piece into a thin log and divide into 6 or 8 pieces, depending on the size of dumplings you want. Lightly flour the divided pieces of dough and roll out each into a thin circle roughly 4 inches in diameter. Keep the dumpling wrappers separated with a small piece of parchment paper, and repeat with remaining dough.

3 Combine cabbage, green onions, garlic, ginger, soy sauce, and sesame oil and mix until well incorporated.

< **SHRIMP**

4 **For the pork filling**, combine the ground pork with the remaining 1 teaspoon salt, the pepper, and 1 cup of the cabbage mixture and stir until well incorporated.

5 **For the veggie filling**, combine the mushrooms and carrot and microwave for 3 minutes, until soft. Add 1 cup of the cabbage mixture and stir until well incorporated.

6 **For the shrimp filling**, combine the shrimp with 1 cup of the cabbage mixture and stir until well incorporated.

7 To assemble the dumplings, add roughly 1 heaping tablespoon of a filling into the center of a dumpling wrapper. With your finger, lightly coat half of the outside of the wrapper with water. Fold the moistened half of the wrapper over the filling and, using a fork, crimp the edges to seal. Repeat with the remaining fillings and wrappers.

8 Heat the oil on medium-high in a large skillet and add a few dumplings, cooking them in batches. Once the bottoms of the dumplings start to brown, add in a splash of water and cover with a lid. Steam for roughly 5 minutes, or until the dumplings are cooked and the water has evaporated. Move the cooked dumplings to a paper towel–lined plate to remove any excess moisture or grease.

9 In a small bowl, combine the soy sauce, rice vinegar, sesame oil, and pepper flakes, and stir to combine. Serve dumplings immediately with dipping sauce.

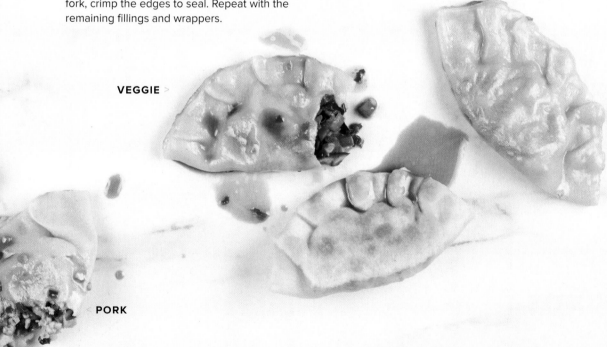

VEGGIE >

PORK

German Pancake (aka Dutch Baby)

SERVES 6

3 **eggs**

1½ tablespoons **granulated sugar**

1 pinch of **salt**

¾ cup **milk**, warm

2 teaspoons **vanilla extract**

¾ cup **all-purpose flour**

3 tablespoons **butter**, 1 tablespoon melted

Powdered sugar, to serve

Sliced **strawberries**, to serve

Puff the magic pancake! Simultaneously eggy, fluffy, and crispy, this confection is more like a giant popover for a crowd. Pour the batter into the frothy hot butter, pop it in the oven, then finish this edible hot-air balloon with fresh fruit and powdered sugar.

1 Preheat the oven to 400°F (200°C).

2 Combine the eggs, granulated sugar, salt, warm milk, vanilla, flour, and 1 tablespoon melted butter in a blender or processor, and mix until smooth.

3 Preheat an oven-safe skillet over medium-high heat for 3 to 4 minutes. Melt the remaining 2 tablespoons butter. Pour the batter into the heated skillet and then immediately, and carefully, move the skillet to the oven and bake for 25 to 30 minutes. It is done when the pancake achieves a rich amber color and the sides have risen considerably. Carefully remove the pancake from the skillet and let cool slightly on a wire rack.

4 Serve warm with powdered sugar and sliced strawberries.

Jamaican Jerk Chicken

SERVES 4

1 whole **chicken**

3 **scotch bonnet** or **habenaro peppers**, seeded and chopped

4 **garlic cloves**, chopped

1 tablespoon fresh **thyme**

1 tablespoon **allspice**

2 **onions**, chopped

1 tablespoon **light brown sugar**

½ tablespoon ground **nutmeg**

½ tablespoon minced **ginger**

1 tablespoon **olive oil**

Juice from 1 **lime**

½ cup **white vinegar**

Salt and **pepper,** to taste

Not only does flattening a whole chicken shorten your total cooking time, but it's all the better for seasoning every nook and cranny of your bird with this tangy, sweet-and-savory blend of spices. Making sure that not even one inch of your chick is neglected makes you anything but a jerk. Use gloves to handle the peppers—they're hot!

1 Prepare the chicken by removing the backbone using a pair of kitchen shears or a sharp knife. Transfer the chicken to a baking sheet and flatten it down to spread the chicken out as much as possible.

2 To a blender or the bowl of a food processor, add the peppers, garlic, thyme, allspice, onions, light brown sugar, nutmeg, ginger, olive oil, lime juice, vinegar, salt, and pepper, and blend until smooth.

3 Pour the marinade over the chicken. Cover with foil or plastic wrap and marinate in the fridge for at least 3 hours or overnight.

4 Preheat the oven to 400°F (200°C).

5 Remove the foil or plastic wrap and bake the chicken for 45 to 50 minutes, until cooked through. Rest for 10 minutes on a cutting board before serving.

Chicken Tikka Masala

SERVES 4 TO 6

CHICKEN MARINADE

3 boneless, skinless **chicken breasts**

½ **cup plain yogurt**

Juice from 1 **lemon**

6 **garlic cloves**, minced

1 tablespoon minced **ginger**

2 teaspoons **salt**

2 teaspoons **cumin powder**

2 teaspoons **garam masala**

2 teaspoons **paprika**

SAUCE

3 tablespoons **oil**

1 large **onion**, chopped finely

2 tablespoons minced **ginger**

8 **garlic cloves**, minced

2 teaspoons **cumin powder**

2 teaspoons **turmeric powder**

2 teaspoons ground **coriander**

2 teaspoons **paprika**

2 teaspoons **chili powder**

2 teaspoons **garam masala**

1 tablespoon **tomato puree**

3½ cups **tomato sauce**

1 cup **heavy cream**

Cilantro leaves, chopped

Bamboo or **wooden skewers**

Once you find out how easy it is to make this rich, tomato-based dish, you may be inclined to take your favorite Indian spot off speed-dial. Serve with rice and naan bread on the side.

1 Preheat the oven to 500°F (260°C). Line a high-sided baking pan or roasting tray with parchment paper.

2 Slice the chicken into bite-sized chunks. Combine the cubed chicken with the yogurt, lemon juice, garlic, ginger, salt, cumin, garam masala, and paprika and stir until well coated.

3 Cover and refrigerate for at least 1 hour, or overnight.

4 Place the marinated chicken pieces on bamboo or wooden skewers, then set them over the prepared baking pan, making sure there is space underneath the chicken to help distribute the heat more evenly. Bake for about 15 minutes, until slightly dark brown on the edges.

5 Make the sauce. Heat the oil in a large pot over medium heat, then sauté the onions, ginger, and garlic until tender but not browned. Add the cumin, turmeric, coriander, paprika, chili powder, and garam masala, and stir constantly for about 30 seconds. Stir in the tomato puree, tomato sauce, and 1¼ cups water, then bring to a boil and cook for about 5 minutes. Pour in the cream.

6 Remove the chicken from the skewers and add to the sauce, cooking for another 1 to 2 minutes. Serve garnished with cilantro.

Rose Dumplings

MAKES 8 DUMPLINGS

FILLING

3½ ounces **shrimp**, cooked and chopped

3½ ounces **ground pork**

2 teaspoons **sake**

Pinch of **salt**

2 teaspoons **soy sauce**

1 teaspoon grated **ginger**

1 **garlic clove**, grated

25 grams (1 ounce) **Chinese chives**, minced

1 teaspoon **sugar**

32 sheets **dumpling wrappers** or **gyoza skins**

2 tablespoons **sesame oil**

SAUCE

2 tablespoons **rice vinegar**

2 tablespoons **soy sauce**

2 tablespoons **chili oil**

These truly do look like flowers when they're done, making them the most romantic item in any dim sum selection. They seem more complicated than they are. Just be sure not to overstuff the dumplings before you fold, seal, and roll—it makes the process more manageable. Word to the wise: You need round dumpling wrappers for this one!

1 In a large bowl, combine the chopped shrimp, ground pork, sake, salt, soy sauce, ginger, garlic, sugar, and Chinese chives, and mix until thoroughly combined.

2 Using your finger, rub the right edge of a dumpling wrapper with water. Lay another dumpling wrapper over the edge, so that it slightly overlaps, sealing tightly. Repeat with 2 more wrappers.

3 Scoop a spoonful of filling onto the middle of each dumpling wrapper. Wet the edge of the wrappers, and fold each wrapper over from top to bottom, ensuring that the edges are still overlapped, sealing tightly. Gently roll the dumplings in a circular shape, starting from the left side, creating a flower shape. Repeat with remaining dumpling wrappers, creating 8 rose dumplings in total.

4 Heat 1 tablespoon of sesame oil in a pan over medium-high heat. Add the dumplings to the pan, and cook for 2 minutes, until the bottoms begin to brown. Add a splash of water to the pan, and put the lid on. Steam for 10 minutes. Remove the lid and drizzle with the remaining tablespoon of sesame oil. Cook on low heat for 3 minutes.

5 In a small bowl, add the sauce ingredients and stir to combine. Remove the dumplings from the pan and serve with the sauce on the side.

Korean BBQ-Style Beef (Bulgogi)

SERVES 2

1½ pounds **rib-eye steak**, or any other well-marbled, tender cut

1 **onion**, half cut into chunks, half cut into thin slices

3 **garlic cloves**

½ **pear**, peeled and cut into chunks

3 **green onions**, 1 cut into pieces, and 2 sliced into ¼-inch rounds

3 tablespoons **brown sugar**

1 teaspoon **black pepper**

⅓ cup **soy sauce**

3 tablespoons **sesame oil**

1 tablespoon **canola oil**

1 teaspoon **sesame seeds**, to serve

Rice, to serve

Korean side dishes (*banchan*), to serve (optional)

Bulgogi (pronounced Bull-GO-ghee) might as well be Korean for delish! Pear is a traditional addition to this sweet-soy situation, helping infuse the meat with its unique flavor profile at warp speed. A quick skillet stir-fry caramelizes the meat as it cooks. Serve it with rice and, if you have access to a Korean restaurant or market, an assortment of pickles and salads called *banchan*.

1 Slice the beef as thinly as you can, then set aside in a large bowl. Using frozen or cold beef makes the slicing easier.

2 In a blender or food processor, blend the onion chunks, garlic, pear, green onion pieces, brown sugar, pepper, soy sauce, and sesame oil until smooth. Pour the marinade over the beef, add the thinly sliced onion, then mix evenly. Cover with plastic wrap and marinate for at least 30 minutes in the fridge, or overnight.

3 Heat the canola oil in a skillet over high heat. Pat the meat dry.

4 Being careful not to crowd the pan, sear the marinated beef and onions until browned. Sprinkle with the slices of green onions and the sesame seeds. Serve with rice and side dishes.

French-Style Apple Tart (Tarte Tatin)

SERVES 4 TO 6

1 sheet **puff pastry**, thawed

6 **apples**, preferably Honeycrisp or Granny Smith

½ cup **sugar**

3 tablespoons **unsalted butter**

Vanilla ice cream, to serve

This one turns the world of apple desserts upside down—literally. Don't wait until it's completely cool before flipping it onto a plate; still warm is where it's at.

1 Using a 9-inch (23-cm) flat-sided cake tin as a template, cut a circle out from the puff pastry. Using a fork, poke holes all over to provide ventilation. Set aside.

2 Peel and quarter the apples, using a spoon or melon baller to remove the core.

3 Preheat the oven to 375°F (190°C).

4 In a large saucepan over medium heat, distribute 3 tablespoons of water and the sugar evenly and cook until a light amber color, stirring to help melt any lumps, 5 to 7 minutes. Add the butter, stirring constantly until the color is a creamy light brown. Add the apples, stirring until they are coated in a thick layer of caramel.

5 Cook for 15 to 20 minutes, making sure the apples are turned constantly so that they bathe in the caramel. Remove from heat when the caramel has reduced and little remains in the bottom of the pan. Be sure not to burn the caramel, tasting it from time to time to ensure it does not taste bitter.

6 Arrange the apple slices in concentric circles on the bottom of the pan. Press the slices tightly against each other, then pour the glaze over the top. Lay the circle of puff pastry on top. Tuck the pastry down the sides of the pan.

7 Bake for 45 to 50 minutes, until the pastry is golden brown and firm. Cool for about 1 hour, then invert onto a plate. Slice and serve with vanilla ice cream.

Sticky Pineapple Chicken

SERVES 2

1 large **pineapple**

2 tablespoons **peanut** or **vegetable oil**

6 boneless, skinless **chicken thighs**, cut into bite-sized cubes

Salt and pepper, to taste

1 tablespoon **hoisin sauce**

1 tablespoon **soy sauce**

1 tablespoon **brown sugar**

1 tablespoon **garlic paste**

½ cup **chicken stock**

Rice, to serve

Sesame seeds, to serve

Basically a tiki party masquerading as a dinner dish, this saucy, tropical chicken uses a pineapple as both its flavor inspiration and serving vehicle. When you buy a whole pineapple, it should smell like a pineapple—that and a nice yellow color peeking through the exterior are telltale signs of ripeness.

1 Using a sharp knife, carefully cut the pineapple in half lengthwise. Using the knife tip, cut around the edge of the pineapple, being careful not to cut through the skin. Slice down and across the pineapple flesh, then scoop out the pineapple cubes with a spoon. Discard the core and set the flesh aside.

2 In a 4-quart jumbo cooker, heat the oil over medium heat. Add the chicken and season with salt and pepper. Fry for about 10 minutes, until browned and cooked through. Remove the chicken and set aside.

3 Add the cubed pineapple, hoisin sauce, soy sauce, brown sugar, and garlic paste and cook for a few minutes. Stir in the chicken stock, bring to a boil, and then simmer, stirring occasionally, until the sauce has reduced and thickened.

4 Put the chicken back in the pan and stir until evenly coated with the sauce. Serve in the empty pineapple halves, along with some rice and sesame seeds.

ON TREND

Cauliflower Crust Pizza Three Ways

EACH SERVES 2

Forget the carb-free angle here: this cauli crust can stand on its own just fine, no matter how you slice it.

CAULIFLOWER PIZZA CRUST

1 head of **cauliflower**, trimmed and cut into pieces

½ teaspoon dried **oregano**

½ teaspoon **garlic powder**

¼ teaspoon **red pepper flakes**

½ teaspoon **sea salt**

¼ cup shredded **Parmesan cheese**

1 large **egg**

PREPARATION

1 Preheat the oven to 450°F (240°C). Line a baking sheet with parchment paper.

2 Add the cauliflower to the bowl of a food processor, and pulse until it becomes the size of rice. Place in a microwave-safe bowl and microwave on high for 3 minutes, or until it begins to steam. Remove the cauliflower and place on a clean kitchen towel. Wrap the towel around it and squeeze out as much liquid as possible; wait for the cauliflower to cool a bit if it's too hot to handle. Transfer the cauliflower to a bowl. Add the oregano, garlic powder, red pepper flakes, salt, Parmesan, and egg. Stir to combine.

3 Transfer the mixture to the baking sheet and use your hands to form it into a round disk, ½ inch (1 cm) thick and 10 inches (25 cm) in diameter. Bake for 25 to 30 minutes, or until the crust begins to brown.

MARGHERITA CAULIFLOWER PIZZA

Cauliflower Pizza Crust (recipe at left)

Marinara sauce

Mozzarella cheese, shredded

4 fresh **basil leaves**

Red pepper flakes, to serve.

1 Preheat the oven to 450°F (240°C).

2 Top the baked pizza crust with marinara sauce, mozzarella, and basil, or other toppings of your choice, and bake for 10 minutes, or until cheese is melted and bubbly. Serve with red pepper flakes.

RAINBOW CAULIFLOWER PIZZA

Pizza sauce

Cauliflower Pizza Crust (recipe opposite)

Mozzarella cheese, shredded

4 **sun-dried tomatoes**

1 **orange bell pepper**, sliced

1 **yellow bell pepper**, sliced

3 ounces prewashed **baby spinach**, chopped

¼ **red onion**, thinly sliced

Grated **Parmesan cheese**, to serve

1 Preheat the oven to 450°F (240°C).

2 Spread a layer of pizza sauce on the baked pizza crust and add the mozzarella. Top with the vegetables. Bake for 8 to 10 minutes, or until the spinach is wilted and the cheese is melted. Serve with grated Parmesan cheese.

PEPPER AND MUSHROOM CAULIFLOWER PIZZA

Cauliflower Pizza Crust (recipe opposite)

1 **green bell pepper**, sliced

6 **mushrooms**, sliced

¼ **red onion**, thinly sliced

10 **cherry tomatoes**, halved

1 Preheat the oven to 450°F (240°C).

2 Top the baked pizza crust with bell pepper, mushrooms, onion, and tomatoes, or other toppings of your choice. Bake for 10 more minutes, or until the tomatoes are bubbly.

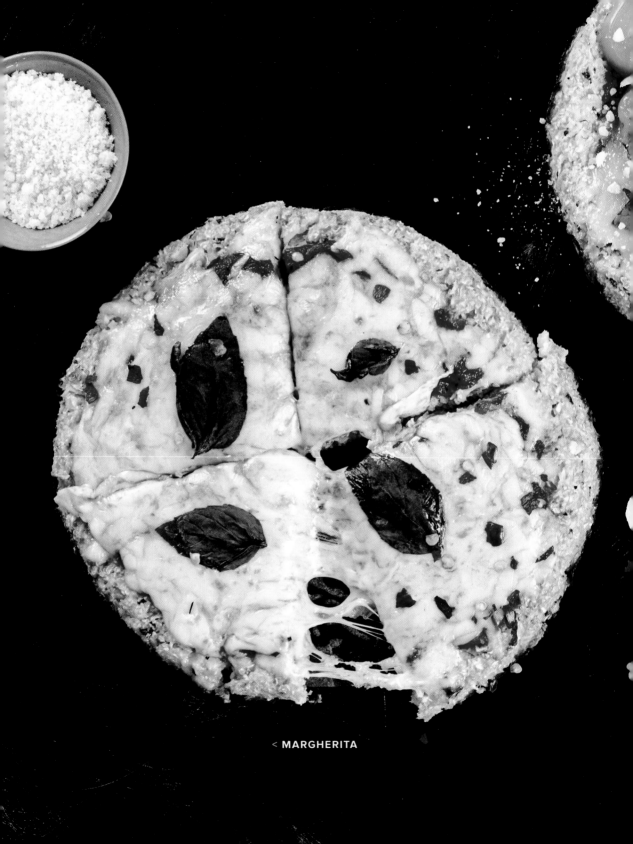

< MARGHERITA

< RAINBOW

**< PEPPER AND
MUSHROOM**

Magic Chocolate Ball

SERVES 2

8 ounces **milk chocolate**, chopped or in chips

2 **brownies**, prepared as desired

Assorted **berries**, to serve

Ice cream, to serve

8 ounces **dark chocolate**, 70% cacao or higher, chopped

1 cup **heavy cream**

SPECIAL EQUIPMENT

6-inch (15-cm) **fillable ornament**, available at craft and baking stores or online

You need one piece of special equipment for this recipe—a fillable ornament—but once you've got that, the rest is relatively easy, and definitely a showstopper.

1 Melt the milk chocolate in a microwave in 20-second intervals, stirring in between each until smooth.

2 Open the ornament, and coat the inside with a lightly oiled paper towel. Pour the chocolate into one of the halves. Close the ornament, rotating the ball so that the chocolate evenly coats the entire surface. Continue slowly rotating for 5 minutes. You may have to shake it a bit to get the chocolate to fill in any holes. Place the ball in the freezer, then flip it after 2 minutes. Continue to flip it every few minutes, 2 or 3 times more. The chocolate should be set by then. Freeze for at least 30 minutes.

3 Remove the ball from the freezer. Carefully open the ornament and remove the ball. Work quickly and avoid touching the ball for too long with your warm hands. If you want to be extra careful, immediately after unmolding, place the ball back into the freezer for a few minutes.

4 Dip or run a flat-bottomed bowl in boiling water, then dry the entire bowl. Invert the bowl onto a flat surface, then place one side of the frozen chocolate ball on the hot bowl.

5 Twist back and forth with a gentle motion, making sure that you're not applying too much pressure. Use a paper towel to help insulate the ball from your warm fingers. You may have to reheat and wipe off the bowl a few times, as it will cool down a bit. Place the ball back in the freezer.

6 On a large plate, stack the brownies on top of each other, then surround them with berries. Place a scoop of ice cream on top of the brownies, then slowly place the chocolate ball on top. To cover up any holes or

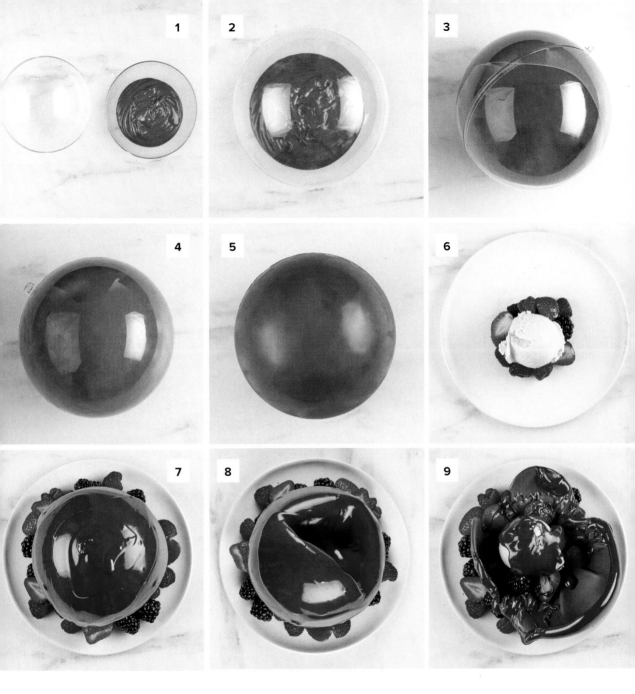

imperfections along the seam of the ball, surround the base of the ball with more berries.

7   Microwave the dark chocolate with the heavy cream in 20-second intervals until smooth and glossy. Pour the chocolate sauce over the ball in a circular motion.

Unicorn Cheesecake

SERVES 8

FILLING

48 ounces **cream cheese**

1 cup **sugar**

2 tablespoons **vanilla extract**

2 cups **warm milk**

2 tablespoons **powdered gelatin**

Food coloring: blue, purple, and pink

CRUST

20 **graham crackers**

4 tablespoons **unsalted butter**

⅓ cup **sugar**

UNICORN HORNS

9 **mini waffle cones**

2 cups **white chocolate**, melted

Sprinkles: pink and blue

FOR SERVING

Sprinkles

Gumballs

Swirl lollipop

Isn't it fun to be living in an age when a full set of food coloring is an essential component of any trendy cook's kitchen? The unicorn phenomenon brings out the inner kid in all of us, allowing us to spread edible fairy dust over all manner of delicious things. Exhibit A: this tricolored cheesecake, which gets topped with little ice-cream cone "horns" and a galaxy of gumballs and sprinkles.

1 Make the filling. In a large bowl, use a handheld mixer to combine the cream cheese, sugar, and vanilla extract. Microwave the milk for 2 minutes, and mix with the gelatin. Add to the cream cheese mixture.

2 Separate the batter into three separate bowls. Add a drop of food coloring to each bowl, and stir to combine.

3 To make the crust, add the graham crackers to a zipper-lock plastic bag, and use a rolling pin to crush until they resemble coarse sand. Transfer to a medium bowl and add the butter and sugar. Mix until thoroughly combined. Press into a greased 8-inch (20-cm) springform pan and chill.

4 Layer the blue batter into the graham cracker crust and refrigerate for 30 minutes, or until firm. Add the purple batter, and refrigerate for 30 minutes. Add the pink batter, and refrigerate for 60 minutes.

5 To make the unicorn horns, dip each waffle cone into the white chocolate, top with sprinkles, and chill until firm.

6 Top the cheesecake with the sprinkles, unicorn horns, gumballs, and the lollipop.

Southwestern Sweet Potato Toast

SERVES 1

1 **sweet potato**

½ small **avocado**

Salt and pepper, to taste

Corn salsa, to serve

Hot sauce, to serve

This stand-in for sliced bread has rapidly moved to the top of the gluten-free pecking order. Not only is it easy, but it doesn't even require a toaster *oven*—just a plain old toaster. Think of this crispy sweet potato base as your palette, your inspo, your canvas waiting to be decorated with salsa (or guac, or yogurt sauce—you get the picture).

1 Cut the sweet potato into thin slices, about ¼ inch (6 mm) thick. Place 1 slice into each slot of the toaster and set it to the maximum cook time. When it pops, flip the sweet potato slices over and toast one more time. Depending on the strength of your toaster and your preferences, you may need to toast it once more. Remove the slices from the toaster and let cool enough to handle.

2 Mash the avocado. Add salt and pepper, and mix until well combined. Spread the mashed avocado evenly across the sweet potato toast, top with corn salsa, and drizzle with hot sauce.

Emoji Fries

SERVES 4

3 **russet potatoes**, peeled and cooked

3 tablespoons **cornstarch**

¼ cup **all-purpose flour**

3 tablespoons **bread crumbs**

1 **egg**

Salt and pepper, to taste

Peanut or **vegetable oil**, for frying

You can never have enough ways to express your emotions. Just in time: Emoji mashed potato fries to the rescue! Just shape the peppery, moldable mixture into little discs, then use a spoon to express your deepest feelings. It's an idea that's so darn cute, you won't know whether to laugh or cry.

1 In a bowl, smash the cooked potatoes with a fork or masher until light and fluffy. Add in the cornstarch, flour, bread crumbs, egg, and salt and pepper, and mix until a slightly crumbly dough forms. Transfer to a floured surface and roll out to about ½ inch (1 cm) thick.

2 With a mason jar lid or cookie cutter, cut out circles from the dough. Shape them into any emoji design you'd like with tools like spoons, straws, toothpicks, forks, and your fingers. Place the shapes onto a baking tray lined with parchment paper and chill in the refrigerator for 30 minutes.

3 Heat the oil in a large, deep pot to 350°F (180°C).

4 Add the emojis and fry for 1 to 2 minutes, or until golden brown. Drain on a paper towel or cooling rack and sprinkle with salt. Serve immediately.

Protein-Packed Buddha Bowl

SERVES 2

MARINADE

2 tablespoons **vegetable oil**

½ teaspoon **sesame oil**

1 teaspoon **hot sauce**

2 teaspoons dried **thyme**

1 teaspoon **paprika**

½ teaspoon **salt**

8 ounces **firm tofu**, drained

1 **sweet potato**, peeled and cubed

1 **onion**, sliced

2 **garlic cloves**, minced

1 tablespoon **peanut** or **vegetable oil**

1 cup **chickpeas**, drained

½ teaspoon **salt**, plus more to taste

½ teaspoon **black pepper**, plus more to taste

1 teaspoon **chili powder**

1 teaspoon **garlic powder**

1½ cups cooked **quinoa**

1 cup **mixed greens** (mesclun greens, baby kale, or spinach would be nice!)

¼ cup shredded **carrots**

1 **avocado**, diced

Juice from 1 **lemon**

This bowl will have you sitting pretty at the lunch table. Loaded with lean protein to power you though the day, its parts can be made ahead of time and stored separately in your fridge. That way, whenever the need arises for a healthy energy supply, you're never more than a bowl away.

1 In a small bowl, whisk the marinade ingredients together to combine. Add the marinade and tofu to a container and refrigerate for at least 30 minutes, or up to a day.

2 Preheat the oven to 400°F (200°C).

3 Lay the sweet potato, onion, and garlic on a baking sheet and drizzle with oil. Season with salt and pepper to taste. Bake for 20 to 25 minutes.

4 In a small bowl, add the chickpeas, ½ teaspoon salt, ½ teaspoon pepper, the chili powder, and garlic powder and stir to combine. Transfer to a skillet and cook over medium heat for about 10 minutes. Set aside.

5 Fry the tofu in the same pan for about 10 minutes on each side. Remove from the heat and slice to your preference.

6 Combine the quinoa, greens, sweet potatoes, onions, chickpeas, carrots, tofu, and avocado in a medium-large bowl, and top off with lemon juice.

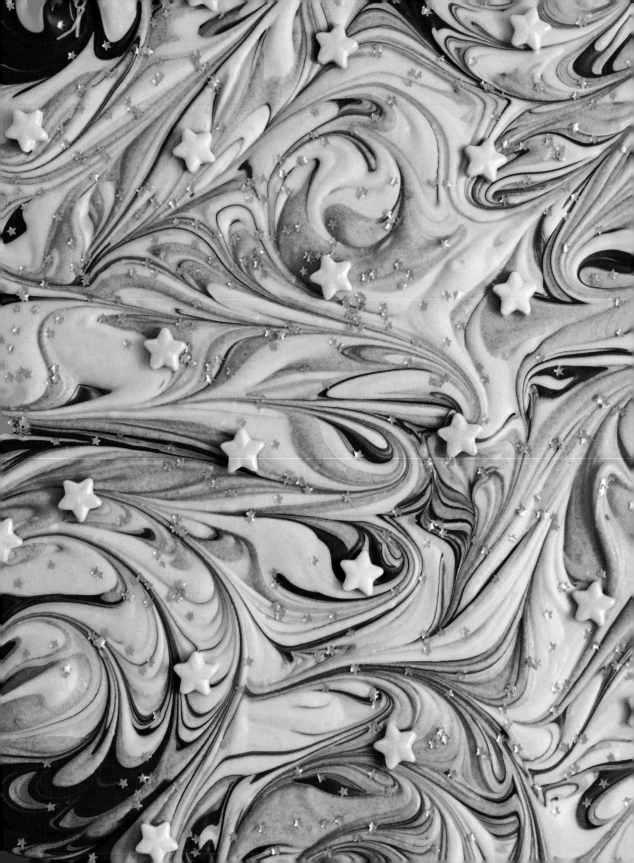

Chocolate Galaxy Bark

MAKES A TRAYFUL

24 ounces **dark chocolate**, chopped or in chips

24 ounces **white chocolate**, chopped or in chips

Food gel: blue and purple

Star spinkles

Mesmerizing to look at and even more intoxicating to eat, this swirly homemade candy will make you feel like a professional chocolatier. Just melt, color, drizzle, and swirl—then decorate the top with little star-shaped confetti sprinkles. Every bite is out of this world.

1 In a large bowl, melt the dark chocolate in the microwave in 20-second intervals, stirring in between each until smooth. Keep warm and set aside.

2 Divide the white chocolate into two separate bowls and melt in the microwave in 20-second intervals, stirring in between each until smooth. Add blue food gel to one and purple food gel to the other until you get the desired color.

3 Line a baking sheet with parchment paper. Pour the dark chocolate on top, using a spatula to spread out to desired thickness.

4 Pour the blue chocolate over the dark chocolate, then add the purple chocolate. Use a knife or skewer to swirl the chocolate around until you get the desired look. Sprinkle with star sprinkles. Refrigerate the chocolate for at least 2 hours before breaking into pieces.

Rainbow Cereal Cheesecake

SERVES 12

10 ounces **marshmallows**

3 tablespoons **butter**

6 cups **fruit-flavored rice cereal**

Peanut or **vegetable oil**, for the pan

16 ounces **cream cheese**, at room temperature

2 tablespoons fresh **lemon juice**

2 cups **heavy cream**

1 teaspoon **vanilla extract**

⅓ cup **sugar**

A crust that tastes like a cross between a fruity bowl of cereal and a rice crispy treat? Check. A dreamy New York–style cheesecake center? Check. The overriding sense of accomplishment when you slice and serve this baby? Well, that's just the sprinkles on this cake.

1 In a large bowl, combine the marshmallows and butter. Microwave for 2 minutes, stirring after 1 minute. Add 5 cups of cereal, and stir until fully mixed. Spoon into the bottom of an oiled 8-inch (20-cm) springform pan, pressing down around the edges to create a smooth surface. Transfer to the refrigerator to chill for about 20 minutes.

2 In a large bowl, whisk the cream cheese and lemon juice until combined. Add the cream, vanilla, and sugar, and mix until it becomes smooth and silky with soft peaks.

3 Pour the cream cheese mixture on top of the rice cereal and marshmallow mix base, using a spatula to create a smooth top. Chill for at least 3 hours.

4 Remove the pan and top with the remaining 1 cup of cereal. Slice and serve.

Zucchini-Noodle Chicken Alfredo

SERVES 2

3 **zucchini**, ends trimmed

2 tablespoons **butter**

2 boneless, skinless **chicken breasts**, thinly sliced

1 teaspoon **kosher salt**

1 teaspoon freshly ground **black pepper**

3 **garlic cloves**, minced

¾ cup **heavy cream**

1 cup shredded **Parmesan cheese**, plus more to serve

2 tablespoons fresh **parsley**, finely chopped, plus more to serve

Zucchini crossed with noodles equals . . . zoodles. Yes, you'll be seeing that word in the next wave of dictionaries. Got a spiralizer? You're in business. No dice? Use a handheld julienne peeler or mandoline for similar results. Just remember that unlike real pasta, you only need to cook these "noodles" for a hot minute.

1 Using a spiralizer, mandoline, or vegetable peeler, turn the zucchini into thin noodles. Microwave the noodles for 1 to 2 minutes, then drain any liquid.

2 Melt the butter in a pan over medium heat. Add the chicken, salt, pepper, and garlic, and cook until the garlic is starting to brown and the chicken is cooked through, about 7 minutes. Remove the chicken from the pan.

3 Add the cream, Parmesan, and parsley to the pan, stirring until evenly combined. Bring to a boil, then stir until the sauce has reduced by about half, 3 to 5 minutes. Put the chicken back in the sauce and stir to coat. Remove from heat and season to taste with salt and pepper.

4 Toss the zucchini noodles with the chicken mixture, and stir until the noodles are coated evenly. Serve with more Parmesan and parsley, if desired.

Fidget Spinner Cookies

FOR 12 COOKIES

2½ cups **all-purpose flour**

¾ cup **sugar**

¼ teaspoon **salt**

1 cup unsalted **butter**, softened

2 teaspoons **vanilla extract**

2 tablespoons **cream cheese**, softened

Royal icing, any color, for decoration

Nothing to be nervous about here: follow the instructions and you'll have an actual working version of our nation's national therapy toy.

1 In a large bowl, add the flour, sugar, and salt, and mix together with a wooden spoon until fully incorporated. Add the butter, and mix until the mixture looks crumbly and slightly wet, about 1 minute longer. Add the vanilla and cream cheese, and mix until dough just begins to form large clumps, about 30 seconds.

2 Transfer the dough to a floured surface and knead until it becomes a cohesive ball. Wrap in plastic wrap and chill in the refrigerator for at least 30 minutes.

3 Preheat the oven to 350°F (180°C). Line a baking sheet with parchment paper.

4 Use a fidget spinner as a guide to cut out 12 shapes in the dough. Use a clean water bottle cap to cut out 12 circles. Take the extra dough and roll out again to ½ inch thickness. With a straw, poke out 12 small pegs that will act as dowels for the fidget spinner cookies.

5 With the same straw, poke holes in the fidget spinner cookie centers and move it around in a circle, widening the hole to be larger than the diameter of the pegs. Place all the shapes on the baking sheet.

6 Bake for 7 minutes and remove the pegs. Rotate the baking sheet and continue baking for 8 minutes, until the cookies are golden brown.

7 Cool the cookies completely, then decorate as you like with your favorite icing or decorations. Use frosting or royal icing as glue to attach a peg to the backside of one of the small circles. Place the fidget spinner cookie base over the peg and attach the second circle cookie with more frosting. Let all the frosting dry before attempting to spin.

BOMBS & RINGS

Stuffed Brownie Truffles Four Ways

EACH MAKES 16 TRUFFLES

The secret to these over-the-top truffles is in the mix. Boxed brownie mix, that is, prepared and rolled around a candy shop's worth of fabulous fillings.

TRUFFLE-STUFFED BROWNIE TRUFFLES

Brownies, prepared

16 **chocolate truffles**

12 ounces **chocolate,** melted

½ cup **cocoa powder**

1 Flip the prepared brownies onto a cutting board. Using a rolling pin, roll out the brownies to about ¼ inch thickness. Cut into 16 equal squares.

2 Wrap one brownie square around each truffle. Seal the truffle completely by rolling it around a few times. Dip each wrapped truffle in melted chocolate, covering the entire ball. Coat in cocoa powder and chill for at least 1 hour, or until ready to serve.

PEANUT BUTTER–STUFFED BROWNIE TRUFFLES

Brownies, prepared

1 cup **peanut butter**

½ cup **powdered sugar**

½ teaspoon **vanilla extract**

½ cup **rice cereal**

12 ounces **chocolate,** melted

¼ cup **peanut butter,** warmed

1 Flip the prepared brownies onto a cutting board. Using a rolling pin, roll out the brownies to about ¼ inch thickness. Cut into 16 equal squares.

2 In a large mixing bowl, combine the peanut butter, powdered sugar, vanilla, and rice cereal. Mix well and freeze for 30 minutes to an hour.

3 Form the peanut butter mixture into 16 equal balls, about 1 teaspoon each. (A melon baller works really well for this.) Wrap a brownie square around each peanut butter ball and roll around to seal. Dip the wrapped truffles in the melted chocolate, covering the entire ball. Using a spoon, drizzle warm peanut butter over the truffles and chill for 30 minutes, or until ready to serve.

COOKIE DOUGH–STUFFED BROWNIE TRUFFLES

Brownies, prepared

1 cup **all-purpose flour**

½ cup **brown sugar**

½ cup **butter**, melted

¼ cup **milk**

½ teaspoon **vanilla extract**

½ teaspoon **salt**

½ cup **mini chocolate chips**

12 ounces **chocolate**, melted

1 Flip the prepared brownies onto a cutting board. Using a rolling pin, roll out the brownies to about ¼ inch thickness. Cut into 16 equal squares.

2 On a small baking sheet, bake the flour at 350°F (180°C) for 5 minutes to kill potential bacteria.

3 In a large mixing bowl, combine the flour, brown sugar, butter, milk, vanilla, salt, and chocolate chips. Mix well and freeze for 30 minutes to an hour.

4 Form the cookie dough into 16 equal balls, about 1 teaspoon each. Wrap a brownie square around each ball of cookie dough. Dip the wrapped truffles in the melted chocolate, covering the entire ball, then chill for 30 minutes, or until ready to serve.

CHEESECAKE-STUFFED BROWNIE TRUFFLES

Brownies, prepared

16 ounces **cream cheese**, softened

1 cup **powdered sugar**

½ teaspoon **vanilla extract**

12 ounces **chocolate**, melted

½ cup **graham cracker crumbs**

1 Flip the prepared brownies onto a cutting board. Using a rolling pin, roll out the brownies to about ¼ inch thickness. Cut into 16 equal squares.

2 In a large mixing bowl, combine the cream cheese, powdered sugar, and vanilla. Mix well and freeze for 30 minutes to an hour.

3 Form the cheesecake mixture into 16 equal balls, about 1 teaspoon each. Wrap a brownie square around each cream cheese ball. Dip the wrapped truffle in the melted chocolate, covering the entire ball. Coat with graham cracker crumbs, and chill for 30 minutes, or until ready to serve.

COOKIE
DOUGH

CHEESECAKE

TRUFFLE

<PEANUT
BUTTER

Blooming Quesadilla Ring

SERVES 20

2 cups cooked and shredded **chicken**

1 **onion**, chopped

1 **red bell pepper**, chopped

1 **jalapeño**, chopped

1 cup **taco sauce**

20 **taco-sized tortillas**

3 cups shredded **cheddar cheese**

3 cups shredded **Monterey Jack cheese**

OPTIONS FOR SERVING

Salsa

Guacamole

Sour cream

Chopped fresh **cilantro**

Quesadilla: Delish, but maybe a bit dull. Blooming quesadilla for a crowd: Delish, and definitely dynamite. Layers of chicken-filled pinwheel cones get stacked, layered with melty cheese, and baked in a circle; pulling them apart produces an Insta-ready stretchy cheese pull. And don't forget to leave room in the middle for the dip—everything's better with sauce.

1 Preheat the oven to 375°F (190°C). Line a baking sheet with parchment paper.

2 In a bowl, add the chicken, onion, red bell pepper, jalapeño, and taco sauce, and mix to combine. Set aside.

3 Cut each tortilla in half. Evenly spread about 2 tablespoons each of the cheddar cheese, Monterey Jack cheese, and chicken mixture on each tortilla half. Roll the tortilla into a cone starting from the cut edge, making sure not to push the ingredients out of the tortilla.

4 Place a wide mouth jar or glass in the center of the baking sheet. Create a ring around the jar with the tortilla cones. The point of the cones should be in the center, touching the jar. There should be about 13 cones in the first layer. Sprinkle both cheddar cheese and Monterey Jack cheese over the layer.

5   Start the second layer of cones by placing 1 cone on top of and in between 2 cones in the first layer. Continue this process with the rest of the cones. There should be 3 full layers of cones with 3 cones left to fill some of the empty space on the top.

6   Sprinkle the rest of the cheddar and Monterey Jack on top of the blooming quesadilla. Remove the jar from the center of the ring. Bake until the cheese is melted and the edges of the tortillas are crispy, 15 to 20 minutes.

7   Carefully transfer the blooming quesadilla to a serving plate. Place your dip of choice inside the ring, and top with desired garnishes. Serve immediately.

Bacon Guacamole Chicken Bombs

MAKES 8 BOMBS

2 **avocadoes**, ripe

½ **white onion**, finely chopped

½ **tomato**, chopped

2 tablespoons fresh **cilantro**, chopped

½ tablespoon **kosher salt**

2 tablespoons fresh **lime juice**

4 boneless, skinless **chicken breasts**

Salt and pepper, to taste

8 **bacon strips**

1 tablespoon **canola oil**

There are never enough ways to (1) use a skinless, boneless chicken breast; (2) eat mashed-up avocadoes; and (3) savor crisp bacon. Thankfully, this recipe allows for all three. Starting this recipe on the stovetop before finishing it in the oven is a restaurant-kitchen trick that ensures a crisp exterior and perfectly cooked, juicy interior.

1 Preheat the oven to 400°F (200°C).

2 Using a knife, cut around the pit of each avocado, separating the halves from each other. Remove the pits and use a spoon to scoop out the flesh.

3 In a large bowl, combine the avocado, onion, tomato, cilantro, salt, and lime juice. Mash and stir with a fork until there are no large chunks of avocado left.

4 Season the chicken breasts with salt and pepper on all sides. Slice in half crosswise. Cut a slit into the center of each half to make a pocket. Take a heaping spoonful of the guacamole and pack it into the pocket. Pinch the edges closed.

5 Wrap each chicken breast with 2 strips of bacon, making sure the ends of the bacon all end up on the same side of the chicken.

6 Heat the oil in a pan over high heat. Sear the bacon-wrapped chicken for 2 to 3 minutes on each side. Remember to sear the sides of the chicken as well. Set the chicken in a baking dish, and bake for 10 minutes, or until cooked through and the internal temperature reaches 165°F (75°C). Serve immediately.

Bangers and Mash Bombs

MAKES 16 BOMBS

3 tablespoons **butter**

1 **onion**, diced

Salt and pepper, to taste

1⅓ pounds **potatoes**, peeled, chopped, and boiled

⅓ cup grated **cheddar cheese**

¼ cup **butter**, softened

8 **pork sausages**, cooked

¾ cup **all-purpose flour**

4 **eggs**, beaten

¾ cup **bread crumbs**

Peanut or **vegetable oil**, for deep frying

Gravy, to serve

There's not a pub in the world that wouldn't want to have these little spud-and-sausage packages on the menu. Encased in a coating of crunchy bread crumbs, they're a great way to use leftover links or mashed potatoes. Serve them with beer at a party, or with a pair of sunny eggs for a killer breakfast.

1 Melt the butter in a small saucepan over medium-low heat. Add the onion, season with salt and pepper, and cook until brown and caramelized, stirring occasionally, about 30 minutes.

2 Mash together the potatoes, caramelized onion, cheese, butter, and salt and pepper. Cut the sausages into 2-inch pieces and encase the sausage in the potato mixture.

3 Lay out three bowls, each containing a different coating: flour, eggs, and bread crumbs. Coat the sausages first in flour, then eggs, followed by bread crumbs, then one more time in the eggs and then the bread crumbs. (In order to reduce mess, maintain one "dry" hand for coating in the flour and bread crumbs and one "wet" for coating in the egg.)

4 Heat the oil in a large pot to 325°F (160°C). If you don't have a thermometer, you can test the oil by dropping in a small piece of white bread. If it sizzles and browns within 45 seconds, the oil is ready.

5 Carefully deep-fry the bangers and mash bombs in small batches for a few minutes until golden brown. Work four at a time so that the temperature of your oil doesn't drop too much. Drain on a paper towel, sprinkle with salt, and serve with warm gravy.

Pizza Bombs

MAKES 16 BOMBS

Butter, for greasing the pan

1 (16.3 ounce) can of **biscuit dough**

8 ounces **marinara sauce**

½ pound sliced **pepperoni**

1 ball **mozzarella cheese,** cut into cubes

3 tablespoons **butter**, melted

2 **garlic cloves**, minced

Salt and pepper, to taste

1 tablespoon **Italian seasoning**

Grated **Parmesan cheese**, for topping

If you were to cross a calzone with a garlic knot, you'd basically end up with these portable mini pizza bombs. The cool hack here is starting with biscuit dough; popping open the can is the gateway to easy filling, formation—and fun. A buttery topping and a sprinkling of Parmesan before baking offer them a brush with greatness. Feel free to customize these bombs with your favorite pizza toppings.

1 Preheat the oven to 375°F (190°C). Line a baking sheet with parchment paper and grease with butter.

2 Cut each biscuit in half. Press each half into a circle with your thumb. Place a small dollop of marinara sauce, 1 pepperoni, and 1 cube of mozzarella on each biscuit round. Bring the edges up and over, pressing them together and being sure to leave no gaps for the filling to leak out. Lay the pizza bombs on the prepared baking sheet.

3 Combine the melted butter, garlic, salt and pepper, and Italian seasoning in a small bowl. Brush the butter mixture onto each pizza bomb and top with Parmesan.

4 Bake for 15 to 20 minutes, or until the bombs have nicely browned. Once they are cool enough to handle, serve.

Neapolitan Brownie Bomb

SERVES 12

2 packages **brownie mix**

⅔ cup **vegetable oil**

2 **eggs**

1½ quarts **strawberry ice cream**, softened

1 quart **vanilla ice cream**, softened

½ quart **chocolate ice cream**, softened

Cocoa powder, to taste

Underneath this dome of goodness lie multiple layers of brownie and ice cream, molded with an assist from nesting bowls. Shaping, filling, and freezing happens in multiple steps, proving that sometimes the most essential ingredient in a recipe is time.

1 Preheat the oven to 350°F (180°C). Line 2 sheet pans with parchment paper and line a large bowl with plastic wrap.

2 In a medium bowl, mix 1 package of the brownie mix, half of the oil, ⅓ cup water, and 1 egg until just combined. Pour the mix into a prepared half sheet pan, and spread with a spatula until even.

3 Repeat with the other brownie mix. Bake both pans for 13 to 15 minutes, until the brownies are fudgy yet firm. Remove from oven and let cool.

4 Once cool, cut one pan of the brownies in half lengthwise, then into 8 equal rectangles. Cut 4 of those rectangles diagonally to make a total of 8 triangles and 4 rectangles. Configure the brownie pieces into the lined bowl so that they cover the sides and bottom. Once the inside is covered, press down firmly on all the brownies, especially the seams, creating a "shell" of brownie. Make sure there are no openings in the outer layer.

5 Scoop the strawberry ice cream onto the brownie shell and smooth with a spatula. Cover with plastic wrap and press a medium-sized bowl into the ice cream, pressing down slightly so that the strawberry ice cream rises up on the sides, and flush with the top of the bowl. Freeze for 3 hours, until the strawberry layer is solid.

6 Unwrap and repeat with the vanilla ice cream, covering it well with plastic and pressing a small bowl into it so that the vanilla ice cream also comes up the sides and is

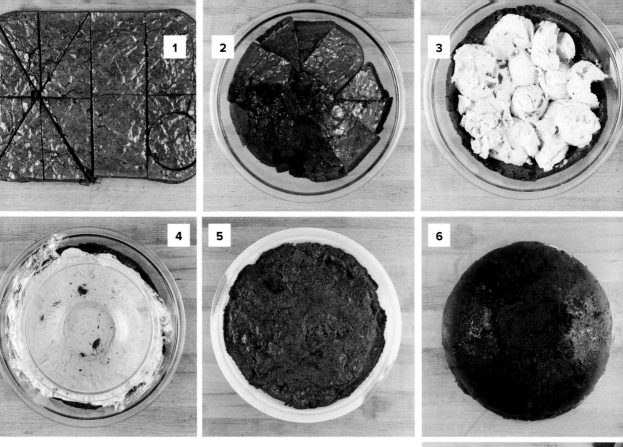

flush with the strawberry layer. Put back in the freezer for another 2 hours.

7 Meanwhile, cut a circle into the other pan of brownies the circumference of the large bowl. This will cover the ice cream layers, creating a base when the bomb is flipped over.

8 Uncover the now frozen vanilla layer, fill the divot with chocolate ice cream, and cover with the cut circle of brownie. (Save the brownie leftovers for later!) Press the circle to secure it, sealing the edges, and freeze the completed bomb for 1 hour.

9 Carefully remove the bomb from the freezer and flip it over onto a cutting board or serving platter. It may need to thaw a couple minutes before it dislodges from the bowl. (Running a warm towel around the bowl will also do the trick.) Once you can lift up the bowl easily, uncover the bomb and dust with cocoa powder.

Cheeseburger Pretzel Bombs

MAKES 14 BOMBS

1 pound **pizza dough**,
left out at room temperature
for 15 to 20 minutes

7 slices of **American cheese**,
cut in half

14 frozen **mini meatballs**,
thawed

¼ cup **baking soda**

1 **egg**, beaten

Coarse sea salt

Yellow mustard, to serve
(optional)

When a recipe looks more complicated than it is but still tastes like a million bucks, you're in a win-win position. These meatball-stuffed, cheese-wrapped cylinders are a great example. The best part is that after making them you'll know how to pretzelize anything you can wrap in plain-old pizza dough; the secret is . . . wait for it . . . baking soda! See recipe for details, then pretzelize to your heart's content.

1 Preheat the oven to 425°F (220°C). Line a baking sheet with parchment paper.

2 Cut the dough into 14 evenly sized pieces. Working one at a time, stretch out a piece of dough into a long strip, about 8 inches (20 cm) long. Place a piece of cheese at the top, followed by a meatball, and roll up the cheese and meatball in the dough. Rotate halfway through rolling to ensure you are completely encasing the cheese and meat into the dough. Pull tightly and use any remaining slack to cover any possible gaps/holes. Press the dough into itself to seal and place on the lined baking sheet. Repeat with remaining dough, cheese, and meatballs.

3 In a medium saucepan over high heat, bring 5 cups of water to a boil. Once boiling, add the baking soda and stir to dissolve. Return the pot to a boil.

4 In batches (working 3 to 5 at a time), add the rolled dough balls into the pot and allow to boil for 20 to 30 seconds, stirring gently. Remove and dab on a paper towel before replacing on the baking sheet. Repeat with the remaining dough balls.

5 Brush each boiled ball with beaten egg and then sprinkle each with coarse sea salt. Bake for 15 to 20 minutes, until the outsides have browned. Serve warm with mustard, if desired.

BBQ Bacon Onion Meatball Bombs

MAKES 8 BOMBS

1 pound **ground beef**

1 teaspoon **garlic powder**

1 teaspoon **onion powder**

1 teaspoon **black pepper**

2 teaspoons **salt**

¼ cup **bread crumbs**

3 **garlic cloves**, minced

½ **onion**, diced

⅓ cup fresh **parsley**, loosely packed

1 **egg**

1 tablespoon **ketchup**

1 tablespoon **mustard**

1 teaspoon **Worcestershire sauce**

1 tablespoon **honey**

4 medium **onions**

8 ounces **cheddar cheese**, cubed

16 strips of **bacon**

16 ounces **barbecue sauce**

Your fridge's condiment shelf provides a wealth of fresh cooking ideas. Yep, we're talkin' barbecue sauce! If you can make a fist, you can form these crazy-good oversized bombs. We call for stuffing them with cheddar, but cheese it up with your favorite variety. There's a bacon wrap, but it's the zing of BBQ flavor that takes these from basic to bomb.

1 Preheat the oven to 425°F (220°C). Line a baking sheet with parchment paper.

2 In a large mixing bowl, combine the ground beef with garlic powder, onion powder, pepper, salt, bread crumbs, garlic, diced onion, parsley, egg, ketchup, mustard, Worcestershire sauce, and honey until evenly combined. Set aside in the refrigerator.

3 Cut the 4 onions vertically on a cutting board. Remove the stem and root from each piece. The layers of each onion will act as "shells" to wrap around each meatball.

4 Remove the meatball mixture from the refrigerator and pinch off a golf ball–sized amount of meat mixture. Press a small cube of cheddar cheese into the middle. Then form into a meatball shape with your hands

5 Wrap each meatball in 2 onion "shells" then in 2 or 3 strips of bacon, securing with a toothpick. Transfer to the baking sheet. Brush the meatballs with barbecue sauce, covering them completely.

6 Bake the meatballs for 45 minutes, or until deep brown with a nice crust on the outside, brushing again with barbecue sauce halfway through baking.

Lasagna Party Ring

SERVES 10

18 **lasagna noodles**

3 tablespoons **canola oil**, plus additional for the baking sheet

½ **onion**, diced

4 **garlic cloves**, minced

¾ pound **80% lean ground beef**

¾ pound **ground sweet Italian sausage**

1 teaspoon **salt**

1 teaspoon **black pepper**

1 (28 ounce) can **crushed tomatoes**

15 ounces **ricotta cheese**

½ cup shredded **Parmesan cheese**

¼ cup fresh **basil**, chopped

1 **egg**

2 cups shredded **mozzarella cheese**

Marinara sauce, to serve

Admit it: those crispy, crusty corners of the lasagna pretty much give you life. If that's the case, prepare for *nine* lives with this version, which puts the noodles, sauce, and cheese into ring formation. Introducing a Bundt pan into the proceedings greatly increases pasta-on-pan contact. So no matter how you slice it, this lasagna's a party.

1 Boil the lasagna noodles in a large pot of salted water, al dente, or 2 minutes shy of the package directions. Drain and lay the cooked noodles on an oiled baking tray, oiling any overlapping noodles to prevent sticking.

2 Preheat the oven to 375°F (190°C).

3 In a large pot over high heat, add the 3 tablespoons oil, the onion, and garlic, and cook until the onion and garlic begin to brown, stirring occasionally, 2 to 3 minutes. Add the beef, sausage, salt, and pepper, and cook, breaking the meat up as you stir, until all of the moisture has evaporated and the meat is starting to brown on the edges, 4 to 5 minutes. Add the tomato sauce, then reduce the heat to a simmer, cooking until the sauce becomes extremely thick, almost paste-like, stirring occasionally, 10 to 15 minutes. Remove from the heat and set aside.

4 In a bowl, combine the ricotta, Parmesan, basil, and egg, mixing until smooth. Set aside.

5 Slice 6 of the lasagna noodles in half. These will serve as the layers in between the meat and the cheese mixture.

6 Spray a Bundt pan with nonstick cooking spray, then lay 12 noodles into the bottom, fanning them out in an overlapping pattern. One end of the noodles should be just as tall as the center of the pan, and the other end of the noodles should hang over the sides.

7 Sprinkle half of the mozzarella into the bottom of the pan on top of the noodles. This will help bind the noodles together when cooked. Spread half of the meat mixture evenly in a ring over the top of the mozzarella, then lay half of the cut noodle pieces over the top to create a noodle layer. Spread all of the ricotta mixture over the noodles in an even ring, then layer with the rest of the noodles and the rest of the meat sauce.

8 Fold the edges of the lasagna noodles hanging over the sides of the pan back toward the center, creating another overlapping pattern. Sprinkle the rest of the mozzarella evenly on top.

9 Bake for approximately 45 minutes, or until the cheese is a deep golden brown. Cool for about an hour, then carefully invert the ring onto a cutting board. Slice the ring, then top with extra Parmesan and basil. Place a small bowl filled with marinara at the center of the ring, for dipping, and serve.

Cheesecake-Stuffed Banana Bread Ring

SERVES 10

CHEESECAKE

16 ounces **cream cheese**, softened

½ cup **powdered sugar**

1 teaspoon **vanilla**

BANANA BREAD

4 ripe **bananas**

1½ cups **all-purpose flour**

½ cup **granulated sugar**

1 teaspoon **baking powder**

4 tablespoons **vegetable oil**

1 **egg**

1 teaspoon **baking soda**

¼ teaspoon **salt**

1 teaspoon **cinnamon**

1 teaspoon **vanilla extract**

CARAMEL

1 cup **granulated sugar**

6 tablespoons **butter**

½ cup **heavy cream**, at room temperature

Oh, hi there, banana bread stuffed with cheesecake and glazed with caramel. Could you possibly be any more addictive? Super-ripe bananas (some brown spots on the skin are totally okay here) will deliver extra-moist cake, and it's shockingly easy to create the cheesecake center. While the cake bakes, boil up the caramel, cool it, and drizzle it on the still-warm cake. (Pssst—the caramel is killer on ice cream, too!)

1 Preheat the oven to 350°F (180°C).

2 In a medium bowl, whisk together the cream cheese, sugar, and vanilla extract, stirring until smooth. Refrigerate.

3 In a large bowl, mash the bananas with a fork. Add in the flour, sugar, baking powder, oil, egg, baking soda, salt, cinnamon, and vanilla. Stir until just combined, without overmixing. Pour half of the batter into a greased Bundt pan.

4 With an ice cream scoop, scoop the cream cheese mixture evenly onto the cake batter in the pan, making sure that it does not touch the sides. Pour the rest of the banana bread batter on top and smooth it evenly. Bake for 30 minutes, or until the banana bread is golden.

5 To make the caramel glaze, heat the sugar in a saucepan over medium-high heat. Once it begins to melt, stir with a wooden spoon or whisk. When it reaches a boil, add the butter and stir until melted. Remove from heat, add in the heavy cream, and immediately stir until incorporated. (Make sure the cream is at room temperature or else it will curdle the sauce.) Allow the caramel to cool and thicken.

6 Invert the banana bread onto a wire rack set on top of a baking tray. Pour the caramel glaze over the cake, letting the excess drip off the wire rack and onto the baking tray. Once the glaze has set, slice the cake.

Thanks to the Tasty staff in 2017 for all you do, all the time.

PRODUCERS
Pierce Abernathy
Hitomi Aihara
Katie Aubin
Adam Bianchi
Brenda Blanco
Mel Boyajian
Betsy Carter
Isabel Castillo
Jody Duits
Daysha Edewi
Joey Firoben
Rachel Gaewski
Andrew Gauthier
Hector Gomez
Crystal Hatch
Andrew Ilnyckyj
Matthew Johnson
Jordan Kenna
Julie Klink
Cyrus Kowsari
Gwenaelle Le Cochennec
Tiffany Lo
Scott Loitsch
Diana Lopez
Rie McClenny
Katie Melody
Nathan Ng
Claire Nolan
Merle O'Neal
Ryan Panlasigui
Greg Perez
Cedee Sandoval
Ochi Scobie
Chris Salicrup
Marie Telling
Alix Traeger
Vaughn Vreeland
Kahnita Wilkerson
Alvin Zhou

PRODUCTION / OPERATIONS / SOCIAL / ADAPTATIONS / VIDSTATS
Maíra Corrêa
Gabi D'Addario
Bryanna Duca
Matt Ford
Nick Guillory
Ashley McCollum
Ryan Mei
Angela Ruffin
Stephen Santayana
Tanner Smith
Nora Snee
Stevie Ward
Lauren Weitz

FOOD
Alexis deBoschnek
Carrie Hildebrand
Claire King
Chloe Morgan
Angie Thomas

BRANDED
Camille Bergerson
Nora Campbell
Sarah Freeark
Robert Gilstrap
Mike Goodman
Liza Kahn
Dylan Keith
Brendan Kelly
Grace Lee
Jess Maroney
Melissa Ng
Ken Orlino
Ryan Panlasigui
Becca Park
Mike Price
Sami Promisloff
Tracy Raetz
Leigh Riemer
Dee Robertson
Katie Schmidbauer
Swasti Shukla
Kate Staben
Allex Tarr
Hannah Williams

INTERNATIONAL
Javier Aceves
Karla Agis
Leticia Almeida
Jordan Ballantine
Guta Batalha
Dani Beck
Matt Cullum
Pierre d'Almeida
Agatha Da Hora
Vanessa Hernandez
Ellie Holland
Sebastian Fiebrig
Daisuke Furuta
Gaspar Jose
Thilo Kasper
Evelyn Liu
Isadora Manzaro
Erich Mendoza
Pierre Michonneau
Daiki Nakagawa
Ryushi Osaki
Lucia Plancarte
Suria Rocha
Gus Serrano
Sonomi Shimada
Toby Stubbs
Yui Takahashi
Jun Tsuboike

Vitor Hugo Tsuru
Nicolas Vendramini
Saki Yamada
Ryo Yamaguchi
Rumi Yamakazi

TECH
Jess Anastasio
Sam Balinghasay
Chad Brady
Fred Diego
Sara Gulotta
Patrick Hernandez
Ryan Inman
Will Kalish
Caitlin Osbahr
Edgar Sanchez
Amir Shaikh
Swati Vauthrin
Graham Wood

Special thanks to Viresh
Chopra

BuzzFeed
PRODUCT
LABS

Thanks to the
bloggers, chefs, and
recipe developers who
get our creative juices
flowing every day.
Specifically, thanks
to these folks, who
inspired some of the
recipes in this book.

Bryon Talbott (Magic
   Chocolate Ball,
   page 146)

Cook's Country (Chicken
   Cordon Bleu, page 74)
Cook's Illustrated (Chicken
   Marsala, page 76, and
   Classic Tomato Lasagna,
   page 78)
Dinner, then Dessert
   (Crispiest Buffalo Wings
   Ever, page 118)
Feeling Foodish (Baked
   Ratatouille, page 100)
Food52 (Barbecue Beer
   Can Chicken, page 35)
Gimme Delicious Food
   (Baked Buffalo
   Cauliflower, page 99)
Haniela's (Fidget Spinner
   Cookies, page 158)
Honestly YUM (Caramel
   Rose Apple Pie, page 59)
Just A Taste (Sticky Pineapple
   Chicken, page 136)
Lindsay Hunt (Chewiest
   Chocolate Chip Cookies
   Ever, page 116)
Little Things (BBQ Bacon
   Onion Meatball Bombs,
   page 178)
Skinnytaste (Zucchini
   "Meat"balls, page 93)
Spend With Pennies
   (Jalapeño Popper Dip,
   page 29)
Spoon University (Emoji
   Fries, page 151)
The Gunny Sack (Slow
   Cooker Beef Stew, page
   83)
The Pioneer Woman (Giant
   Cinnamon Roll, page 52)
Tori Avery (Falafel, page 94)
Wholefully (Softest Sugar
   Cookies Ever, page 113)

Thanks to everyone
at Clarkson Potter for
their vision, agility, and
dedication.

Amanda Englander
Stephanie Huntwork
Jan Derevjanik
Chloe Aryeh
Mark McCauslin
Philip Leung
Kelli Tokos
Alexandria Martinez
Merri Ann Morrell
Linnea Knollmueller
Derek Gullino
Aislinn Belton
Kate Tyler
Carly Gorga
Erica Gelbard
Aaron Wehner
Doris Cooper
Gabrielle Van Tassel
Jill Flaxman
Katie Ziga
Christine Edwards

Thanks to our photo
team for making us
look really, really
ridiculously good.

Lauren Volo
Molly Schuster
Maeve Sheridan
Christina Zhang
Jacklyn Reid
Joy Howard
Brianna Ashby
Jenifer Pantano
Greg Wright
Andie McMahon

Index